Early Praise for *Sweet Marjoram*

True wisdom and beauty, in a time when we dearly need both.

—Eileen Pollack, author of *The Bible of Dirty Jokes*

One could place this book, so different from its contemporaries, in the dive-in-get-wet tradition begun by Montaigne: choose a subject as your starting point and then follow where your musings take you. But I am reminded of another French thinker as well, the philosopher of the imagination Gaston Bachelard, who reminded us that "Words dream." In *Sweet Marjoram,* DeWitt Henry leans in close, divines those dreams, follows their lyrical and associative reasoning, and in his precise and luminous prose, maps our contemporary consciousness, noting our psychic landmarks, our moral architecture, the roads we take to the things that matter.

- -Richard Hoffman, author of *Half the House* and *Love & Fury*

Be warned! The far-ranging notes and essays of *Sweet Marjoram* are addictive. Once I began reading, I couldn't stop. I wanted more of Henry's wit and wisdom, his dazzling, surprising juxtapositions. I wanted to see him keep making the familiar new, and the strange familiar. Whether he's writing about folly or time or food or meat or envy or appetite, Henry has a gift for making his reader see the world afresh. A delightful and highly original collection.

—Margot Livesey, author of *Mercury* and *The Hidden Machinery*

In case anyone is still wondering about the accrued benefits of a lifetime's reading, teaching, viewing and thinking, DeWitt Henry's *Sweet Marjoram* offers the spirited and enjoyable answer. A Shakespearean breadth of interest subjected to a steady inquiring pressure—the reader finds aphorisms for living on every page.

—Sven Birkerts, author of *Changing the Subject: Art and Attention in the Internet Age*

This book is a tasting. Taste a glass of wine and you discover aromas and flavors. Taste a pastry dipped in tea and you may lose yourself in a flood of memories. Open this book, pore over it, dip into it, and you do both with words and ideas: every page wreaths your mind in images, imaginings, allusions, illusions, and recollections.

—JAMES HARBECK, blogger at Sesquiotica
and author of *Confessions of a Word Lush*

SWEET MARJORAM:
NOTES & ESSAYS

DeWitt Henry

a plume editions book

AN IMPRINT OF MADHAT PRESS
ASHEVILLE, NORTH CAROLINA

MadHat Press
MadHat Incorporated
PO Box 8364, Asheville, NC 28814

The Library of Congress has assigned
this edition a Control Number of
2018948910

ISBN 978-1-941196-72-4 (paperback)

Text by DeWitt Henry
Cover image by Marc Vincenz
Cover design by Marc Vincenz

Plume Editions
an imprint of MadHat Press
www.MadHat-Press.com

First Printing

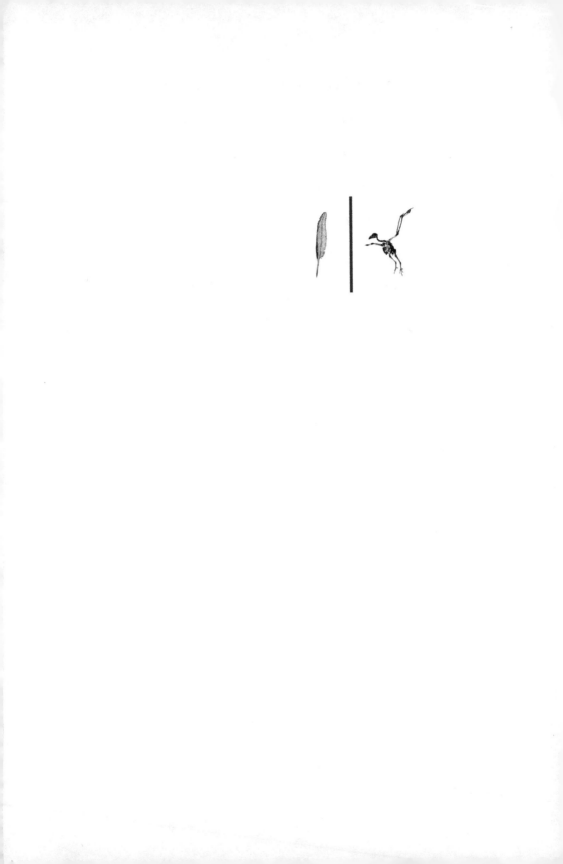

Also by DeWitt Henry

Falling: Six Stories, 2016 (fiction)

Visions of a Wayne Childhood, 2012 (memoir)

Sweet Dreams: A Family History, 2011 (memoir)

Safe Suicide: Essays, Narratives, and Meditations, 2008 (memoir)

The Marriage of Anna Maye Potts, 2001 (novel)

Sorrow's Company: Writers on Loss and Grief, 2001 (editor)

Breaking Into Print: Early Stories and Insights into Getting Published: A Ploughshares anthology, 2000 (editor)

Fathering Daughters: Reflections by Men, 1998 (co-editor with James Alan McPherson)

Other Sides of Silence: New Fiction from Ploughshares, 1993 (editor)

The Ploughshares Reader: New Fiction for the Eighties, 1984 (editor)

For John Skoyles

Table of Contents

Lear: Ha! Give the word.
Edgar: Sweet marjoram.
Lear: Pass.
—*King Lear* (4.6.93–95)

On Weather

Suzanne Langer observed in 1941, the year that I was born, that city dwellers have lost touch with the elements: "We have put many stages of artifice and device … between ourselves and the rest of nature. The ordinary city dweller knows nothing of the earth's productivity; he does not know the sunrise and rarely notices when the sun sets; ask him in what phase the moon is, or when the tide in the harbor is high, or even how high the average tide runs, and likely as not he cannot answer you. Seed-time and harvest are nothing to him. If he has never witnessed an earthquake, a great flood, or a hurricane, he probably does not the feel the power of nature as a reality surrounding his life at all. His realities are the motors that run elevators, subway trains, and cars, the steady feed of water and gas through the mains and of electricity over the wire, the crates of foodstuff that arrive by night and are spread for his inspection before the day begins, the concrete and brick, bright steel and dingy woodwork that take the place of earth and waterside and sheltering roof for him. His 'house' is an apartment in the great man-made city; so far as he is concerned, it has only an interior, no exterior of its own. It could not collapse, let in rain or blow away. If it leaks the fault is with a pipe or with the people upstairs, not with heaven…." (*Philosophy In A New Key*).

The novels of Elizabeth Bowen, especially *The Death of the Heart*, make a similar point as her characters rely on interior decorating for "symbols" in a way that echoes the Romantic poets' use of nature.

Weather forecasts are versions of fortune telling. We plan our dress, our raingear, our travel according to predictions from anywhere to hours to days ahead. The forecasters tell of high-pressure centers and low-pressure centers. Computer models predict how these atmospheric eddies drift and swirl. Orbiting weather satellites transmit pictures from outer space showing storm patterns, drought patterns, and other data. More often than not our TV weather predictions prove accurate,

1

but not always. Based less on meteorology and more on hearsay hunches, *The Old Farmer's Almanac* presumes to predict weather a year ahead of time: hot summer, mild winter. I love the joke of the home weather gauge that consists of no more than a horse's tail with the legend: "when wet, it's raining; when dry, it's not."

Fortune depends on probabilities and likelihoods. We can make choices to avoid risk or to minimize bad luck. Hence we save for a rainy day. We get insurance. We can buckle our safety belts, sneeze into our elbows, drive posted speed limits, ban guns, use condoms. Fate, perhaps like climate, is fixed.

Inner and outer weather: inner, in the poet's sense, is emotional: "Oh let me not go mad!"

"Nice day!" I greet my neighbor, Ron, with whom I have little other concerns in common. This we can agree on. Weather serves for small talk.

Halcyon days!

On a clear day you can see forever.

Fair-weather friends. Where everything is favorable and possible, people support you; but when the going gets rough, they desert.

A person for all seasons weathers circumstance.

Weather vane is weather vain.

Inclement weather, like sickness, is merciless, without pity.

Natural disasters: floods, earthquakes, tsunamis, tornadoes, hurricanes; all call for decency and fellow feeling (all cruels else subscribe).

To everything there is a season.

Wait an hour and the weather will change.

If our stream rises, then our neighbor must have gotten rain.

We pray for weather, especially rain for crops. Rainmakers sow the clouds with salt. Farmers irrigate with giant, overlapping sprinklers. Snow-making machines crystallize water and blow it out on ski trails. In winter, we hover around the hearth; in summer, the a/c. Birds migrate, as do retirees, from climate to climate. From mid-winter Boston, first gasp of tropical heat and humidity as we deplane in Cartagena, parkas in arms.

Landscape weathers, the Appalachians once as mighty as the Rockies. We study geological time: tectonic plates colliding; continental drift.

Acid rain eats away the Parthenon. Carbon dioxide warms the atmosphere. The ice caps melt. Ocean levels rise. Developed nations seek to conserve energy, scrub smoke from the burning of coal, reduce our carbon footprint, but others do not. Nuclear plants have meltdowns, contaminants, and emissions. We look instead to biomass, wind, solar, geothermal and hydroelectric sources, harvesting kilowatts. Our deserts are forested by wind turbines and covered by acres of solar panels.

Global weather is only local on the cosmic scale. We see our planet from the moon. Our probes photograph Jupiter's spot, a hurricane. The Mars rover sends back data from a dust storm. Sun spots are storms. Solar flares send out a wind that is bent by our magnetic field, resulting in radio interference and the Northern Lights.

It's overcast and 800 degrees on Venus.

Space weather! Geomagnetic storms! This universe that we study, probe, and dream remains as baffling to us as it was to Galileo, Aristotle, the Aztecs, or the Druids. Its weathers contain and condition us. Our

3

science is an idiom of faith. Tzimtzum: "God began the process of creation by 'contracting' his infinite light in order to allow for [an] … 'empty space' in which spiritual and physical worlds and ultimately free will can exist" (quoth Wikipedia).

The Old Testament God wielded extreme weather to purge us of idolatry; only the chosen survived with the rainbow as a covenant. Hollywood's sci-fi imagines an ark in space.

Prospero's Tempest: that perfect storm of art, providential or vengeful, and the effort of the beating mind. Or Alice Munro (in "The Moons of Jupiter," 1983), writing of planetariums: "The ones who promoted this show, weren't they immune themselves to the extent that they could in the echo-chamber effects, the music, the church-like solemnity, simulate the awe that they supposed they ought to feel? Awe—what was that supposed to be? A fit of the shivers when you looked out the window? Once you knew what it was, you wouldn't be courting it."

If not all, the readiness is something. Here, try my invisible umbrella, whose force field deflects the rain. "My mother told me, always take your rubbers off in the house!" raved my friend, that stormy day of another psychotic episode.

Mark Strand: "They moved beyond the claims of weather."

On Conscience

"The aginbite of inwit," Richard Rolle of Hampole called it. Prick of conscience. The voice of God within. Internal wisdom.

Tolstoy saw most people seeking to silence it with habit, if not with tobacco, alcohol, and other drugs. See "Why Do Men Stupefy Themselves?": "The cause of the world-wide consumption of hashish, opium, wine, and tobacco, lies not in the taste, nor in any pleasure, recreation, or mirth they afford, but simply in man's need to hide from himself the demands of conscience."

We speak of social conscience. Of artistic conscience.

Joyce ends his *Portrait of The Artist* with Stephen Dedalus's vow to "forge the uncreated conscience of my race."

I love the witty dismissal by Shakespeare's Second Murderer (a hit man) in *Richard III*: "I'll not meddle with it; it makes a man a coward. A man cannot steal but it accuseth him; a man cannot swear, but it checks him; a man cannot lie with his neighbor's wife, but it detects him. 'Tis a blushing shamefaced spirit that mutinies in a man's bosom. It fills a man with obstacles. It made me once restore a purse of gold that, by chance, I found. It beggars any man that keeps it. It is turned out of towns and cities for a dangerous thing, and every man that means to live well endeavors to trust to himself and live without it."

Its legacy is shame. "The worm of conscience still begnaw thy soul."

"Oh, shame, where is thy blush?"

Jiminy Cricket to Pinocchio: "Yep, the world is full of temptations.... They're the wrong things that seem right at the time. But sometime the wrong things may be right at the wrong time or vice versa.... Understand...? Give a little whistle and always let your conscience be your guide."

Clear conscience. Troubled. Weighing on. Strong. Weak. Stirrings of. Haunted by.

Tim O'Brien: "I felt guilty for my conscience." How to resolve divided duties? Conscientious objection? Drafted, we believe our country's policies unjust. Social conscience is conflicted by moral conscience.

Abraham proceeds to sacrifice Isaac.

Freud called it the superego. Inherent? Learned? Think psychopaths and sociopaths. How could he, a teenager, mow down children at Sandy Hook? The abused abuse. The motiveless malignity.

Beyond good and evil, writes Nietzsche. Banality of evil, says Hannah Arendt. Rebel conscience, says Camus. Saint Genet, the criminal, says Sartre.

Wired for righteousness. Suicide bombers. Kamikazes.

Animals have instincts. In humans, conscience overrules instinct. Or tries to. We can't afford that iPhone, but don't reach out to steal it.

Ten Commandments. 613 mitzvoth. Sharia. Taboos: Acts, Persons, Things, Words. Nemesis.

Embarrassed by thanks for our spontaneous generosity, we say "Pass it on." Or some of us do.

Sometimes.

On Falling

Leaves fall, blazing. From spring buds to green, spread-veined leaves, transforming light into energy until the sun lowers, temperatures drop, birds migrate, veins wither, greens fade to yellows and reds, pliant turns brittle, stalks snap, dead leaves spin and flutter down. Fall.

Fortune's wheel, the zeniths and nadirs; the fall of kings as Medieval tragedy. *De Casibus.* From power and esteem (self and otherwise); from grace. Downfall. Comedown.

Lucifer's fall. Fallen angels, wings clipped. "Hurled headlong flaming from the Ethereal Sky / With Hideous ruin and combustion down," sings Milton.

The fall of man; original lapse. Eve's appetite. Knowledge is guilt. Driven Eastward.

Alice falls down the rabbit hole, falls and falls.

Horatio's vertigo: "The very place puts toys of desperation / Without more motive, into every brain / That looks so many fathoms to the sea / And hears it roar beneath." Gloucester pratfalls, blindly, from imagination's heights.

The suicide's fall, from bridge or window ledge.

The hanged man's, to the end of his rope.

The jumper's fall from the Trade Center, tumbling. From fire into the void. For how many seconds? Seven? Ten?

Window washer's, as his scaffold slips.

Icarus's, with melting wings.

The runner's fall, tripped by a root and stumbling in midstride, out of control, knowing in slow motion the certain disaster, happening, as asphalt rises to impact, hands brace, shoulder turns, then head smacks, like Marciano's to Walcott's fist.

Galileo's Law of Fall. The speed of a falling body is independent of its weight. All falling objects accelerate at 9.81 meters per second per second. Dropped together, a feather and hammer (air resistance excepted) should strike the ground simultaneously.

The tandem skydive from 15,000 feet. Bodies harnessed together for dear life, the neophyte's and instructor's. Goggles for the wind. Jump suits rippling. For 60 seconds "more like flying than falling," attaining a terminal velocity of 120 mph before the ripcord's pull, the bloom and jolt of the rainbow-colored canopy; then five more minutes, floating to the ground.

Five show jumpers plunge and maneuver to join hands in mid-air, spread-eagled and knees bent, before they separate and their chutes trail, ripple out and fill.

On Youtube, headset cams record each of two daredevils wearing webbed gliding suits. They leap, one after the other, from a mountain peak into updrafts and soar down over cliffs and ridges, over tree tops, riding the wind, until far below a valley greatens. Then open their parachutes for landings, running. Leonardo's dream turned sport.

Flight is careful falling, riding air.

The bungee cord's elastic limit, its rescuing heave, then down again, then up, resilient, fading.

Falling in love, attracted as if by natural law and fate.

Fallen soldiers; fallen civilizations, Aztec, Egyptian, Roman.

The Dow falls, stocks lessen. Lungs rise, fall.

Possessions fall. The precious bowl, escaped from hands, turns in mid-air beyond reclaim.

Our planet drifts, spinning, pulling with its gravity and pulled by the sun's.

Free fall. Astronauts weightless, ricochet from padded walls.

The Runner picks himself up, no broken bones or blood; walks stiffly, then keeps jogging.

The fallen king discovers wisdom, humility, and compassion.

Spring buds return.

My wife revises, "Down will come baby, cradle and all" to "Down will come baby, into Mommy's arms."

On Handshakes

There are firm ones. Soft, almost boneless ones. Hardy/hearty ones. Two-handed ones, cocooning. Congratulatory ones (well done!). Business ones, the deal settled. Kinship ones. Secret, coded ones for fraternities and special groups. Ones for greeting and for farewell. Ones for reconciliation, after fights.

Less than hugs, but sometimes prelude to one, with pats on the back.

"Forgive me for not shaking hands," says the mechanic, hands smeared with oil and grease. Rough hands, thick and calloused. Delicate hands, protected by gloves. Warm hands, cold. A gesture of peace, perhaps, by hands without weapons.

One recent variation is the fist-bump, knuckles to knuckles (which probably mimics fighters touching gloves before and after bouts).

Another, the prankster's, is hiding a buzzer in the palm; or suddenly jerking back the hand, just before the clasp.

More elaborate are hand kisses, in the high European style. The lady extends her hand, palm down, and the gentleman (never a lady) touches her fingers with his lips. This implies respect to the lady, if not adoration and obeisance.

Different cultures shake with different meanings. In Russia, a man who shakes a woman's hand, instead of kissing it, is seen as impolite (except in business deals, where shaking is expected). Moroccans greet with a kiss on each cheek or after shaking, place the palm on the heart. Weak handshakes are best in Japan, China, and South Korea; firm ones in Norway. Hindis give a slight bow with hands pressed together, palms touching, meaning to convey "I bow to the divine in you."

Tickling a shakee's hand with the middle finger is an invitation to sex.

"Palm to palm is palmer's kiss."

Press the flesh.

Islam discourages handshakes between men and women, probably to ensure chastity. In Switzerland, when an Imam's sons recently refused to shake their teacher's hand—a Swiss tradition—authorities imposed a $5000 fine and provoked an international controversy. The boys had protested that "shaking a female teacher's hand was against their beliefs as Muslims because physical contact with the opposite sex is allowed only to family members" (*USA Today*, 5/26/16). Deedra Abboud, a convert to Islam, sees the Swiss response as intolerant. To shake or not is a personal choice, she insists. She worries about girls discontinuing school or participating in society in order to avoid the physical touch requirement. Instead, she advises men to ask permission of Muslim women before offering to shake. Also observant Muslim women can wear gloves, if need be; or hold their hands behind their back. She herself has shaken hands with men in Muslim countries, and has relaxed the rule in her Western business life. "As societies become more diverse, even without immigration, some traditions will survive and some will not. Mostly it will depend on the reasons behind the traditions and how well those ideas are articulated as valuable and relevant to an ever-evolving world" (http://www.blogher.com/should-traditions-trump-personal-choices).

In addition to religious customs, there are also health and safety concerns. Handshakes spread germs. No one shook on deals with the germophobe Howard Hughes. Supermarkets offer wipes to sanitize shopping cart handles as a precaution against epidemics of flu or AIDS. Dentists and doctors wear latex gloves to protect them from our bodily fluids and us from theirs. Gyms request that users wipe down equipment. Schools dispense wipes to protect against germs, which can be transmitted on door handles, on railings, on desks and keyboards. Students and teachers are cautioned to wash their hands often. And toll collectors? Some wear gloves, some don't. Most toll payers do not. And money itself?

We ask for a woman's (or partner's) hand in marriage. "Dear Isabel," announces *Measure for Measure*'s Duke to the novice nun, "I have a motion much imports your good." She remains silent, but usually they exit hand in hand.

We hold hands, or walk hand in hand, for belonging, for comfort, for safety.

Give me a hand, we say; or in extremis, rescue me.

In "Hands Across Catholic America," Andrew Santella writes: "In many churches it has become standard practice for churchgoers to hold hands with their neighbors as they pray the Our Father, sometimes reaching across aisles and over pew-backs to do so. Hand-holders say the practice is all about community and fellowship and unity. (It's called the Our Father, they like to say, not the My Father.) But to some old-school Catholics, hand-holding detracts from the solemnity of the Mass and the sober mysteries of Catholic tradition." (http://www.slate.com/articles/life/faithbased/2005/10/hands_across_catholic_america.html).

As we filed out of church in my boyhood, our Presbyterian minister stood at the rear shaking hands like a party host.

The young John Keats's last fragment:

> This living hand, now warm and capable
> Of earnest grasping, would, if it were cold
> And in the icy silence of the tomb,
> So haunt thy days and chill thy dreaming nights
> That thou would wish thine own heart dry of blood

So in my veins red life might stream again,
And thou be conscience-calmed—see here it is—
I hold it towards you.

Edward Hirsch comments: "He [the poet] once lifted up a living hand. It reaches out to us still, but now through words. Here it is—this made work, this living thing. Look, he is holding out his hand. He is challenging you, whoever you are, to grasp it." (https://www.poetrysociety.org/psa/poetry/crossroads/old_school/on_john_keats_this_living_hand/)

On Silence

The racket of birdsong wakes me at 4 a.m., before first light.

"Music in the Morning" on WGBH regularly opened with five minutes of recorded birdsong, beginning with one or two birds, then growing to a chorus of warbles, cries, and chirps that merged gradually into an instrumental symphony, by Mozart, I think.

Lightning flash! Count seconds, 4, 5, thunderclap! The distant batter hits the ball; he's already running, when I hear the ping. Sound travels at 1087 feet per second at sea level. If we travel faster than 600 mph, via jet or rocket, we break the sound barrier. Groundlings hear a sonic boom. Under water, sound slows. Think sonar pings or whale songs.

We had a game in camp: I whispered through cupped hands into one side of a curved, empty swimming pool and my friend heard on the other, a variation of echo.

I listen through motel plasterboard, ear to the base of a drinking glass. Or if the noise of TV, sex, hilarity, or fight is too loud, I push in rubber ear plugs. Pillow over my head.

Expensive ear-muffs, like headsets, are required for shooters, for jack-hammerers, for jetliner ground-crew people and baggage handlers.

Remember from biology? The eardrum. Tympani. Middle ear. Inner ear. The little bones and fluid. The hammer, anvil, stirrup, the cochlea, the auditory nerve.

Clean out your ears!

I wince in high-school shop each time my hammer hits the copper bowl I shape on an anvil. I can't help myself.

There is no absence of sound, except to the deaf, who feel vibrations through the floor or other surfaces by touch.

Buddhist teasers: The sound of one hand clapping. A tree falls in an empty forest. Sunyata.

Listen carefully, and even in scientifically designed anechoic chambers, in the absence of most sound, you'll hear the roar and pulse of your own blood. (This, of course, is amplified in ultrasound exams of the heart, which, when I heard mine from a speaker, sounded like kicking in a bath, glug, wash, glug.)

Our industrial and technological revolutions have increased ambient noise, especially in cities. Steam locomotives and steam engines. Factories and mills. Later: cars, trucks, buses; prop planes overhead and the rumbling of jets. Subways rattling and squealing. Pile drivers. Sirens, whistles, horns. The churn and wheeze of sanitation trucks. Fire-engines. Radios, sound systems and TVs. "The din of man," George Michelsen Foy calls it.

We amplify our sounds: on our own, from whisper to shout, or with cupped hands or megaphone, or with the help of electronics. Through our floor, the downstairs child booms on his father's mic: "I got a BIG voice!" My car radio, tuned reasonably, plays jazz, while the dude's or jane's car nearby booms out full-volume rap. We fight to sleep, while neighbors laugh, shout, shriek and dance, at least until the cops arrive.

Legislation limits airplane noise over neighborhoods near airports. New York City passes noise ordinances. No honking. Your muffler, fix it. Amtrak provides special Quiet Cars, no cell phones (that is, no one-sided, private conversations, aloud) allowed.

A femme fatale once told me that when she'd cried as a child, her father had shut her in the basement; so she'd been trying to wake up men ever since.

Hearing aids turn up sound for the hard of hearing, while for the hearing, over-amplification can lead to hearing loss. An ad for high-end speakers shows a listener gripping his chair arms, with his hair and tie blown back.

My neighbor's chained shepherd kept haranguing me, until finally I recorded his bark on my digital recorder. Next time he started, I played it back at him, full-volume, thinking of RCA's trademark, "His master's voice." He promptly stopped and looked puzzled. Whatever he'd been calling me, now he'd been called back in kind.

From the Arecibo dish-telescope in Puerto Rico (1000 feet in diameter), we transmit signals into deep space, announcing ourselves; and listen, so far in vain, for incoming signals.

Speak now, we say, or forever hold your peace.

Enfolding silence, thick silence, heavy; moments filled with silence.

Dead silence.

We mute the TV during the familiar, annoying commercial.

Philomela, the rape victim, tongue-less, hand-less.

Br'er Rabbit and Tarbaby.

Hold your tongue.

Tongue-tied?

Dip your tongue in the honey of your mind before speaking.

Make him talk. Waterboard her.

Priests and shrinks can't reveal our secrets. Vows of silence. Gag orders.

The silent treatment.

Deep throat.

Join the march to have our voices heard.

Walt Whitman, barbaric yawper, heard America singing.

"I had nothing to say and I am saying it," said John Cage.

On Dignity

It's an idea, dignity. An idea or *image* of our kind.

The idea has its history, varying from pride to humility to self-contempt.

Ancient heroes had dignity, larger than life. Achilles, Hector, Priam, Aeneas; also Medea, Electra, Dido. Aristotle explains the tragic hero as "a man not superlatively good and just, not yet one whose misfortune comes about through vice and depravity; but a man who is brought low through some error of judgment or shortcoming." Nobility is brought to nemesis, usually by excessive pride, or hubris.

The Bible emphasizes man's first disobedience, and subsequently her/his punishment for sin and vanity. The followers of false gods, the blasphemous and vain suffer destruction, whether Egypt's kin or the revelers of Sodom and Gomorrah. Yet the chosen, the pious, the wise stand as our exemplars. Noah, Moses, Solomon, David, Job,and the New Testament Jesus. Heroes give way to saints, virtus to virtue, greatness to goodness.

If we choose and shape our destinies, then we portray our bodies as heroic, as in Michaelangelo's outsized statue of David; if, on the contrary, we submit to powers greater than ourselves, then we sculpt our bodies as small, grotesque, cramped, and crushed by burdens, as in Medieval sculpture. Are we glorious, or are we wretched?

Renaissance philosophy argues for glorious. Pico della Mirandela's "Oration on the Dignity of Man," for instance, surveys the Great Chain of Being and sees man as "wondrous" because 1) God made him in his own image and 2) placed him in the middle: "We have made you neither of heavenly, nor of earthly stuff, neither mortal nor immortal, so that with free choice and dignity, you may fashion yourself into whatever form you choose. To you is granted the power of degrading yourself into the lower forms of life, the beasts, and to you is granted the power, contained in your intellect and judgment, to be reborn into the higher forms, the divine." Man is "the great shape-shifter."

Mid-play, W. S.'s Hamlet takes a soured view: "What a piece of work is a man, how noble in reason, how infinite in faculties, in form and moving how express and admirable, in action how like an angel, in apprehension how like a god—the beauty of the world, the paragon of animals! And yet, to me, what is this quintessence of dust?"

Fathers and exemplars die. Death levels all mortals, from Falstaff to Hotspur. But esteem too is personal. Subjectively we glamorize, as Hamlet does his father, or Ophelia and Laertes do Polonius. "A beast that wants discourse of reason would have mourned longer," complains Hamlet of his mother. Our private need for value is contradicted by others' indifference.

What about beasts? Darwin dismisses religious notions, but agrees that we are the highest form of animals. We're distinguished from lower animals, not only as featherless, relatively hairless bipeds with broad nails, but also by the size and complexity of our brains. Thanks to eons of natural selection, we've progressed from apes to Neanderthals to Cro-Magnons, to us. We use tools, etc. We think we're the only animals capable of thought and speech, give or take whale songs and Koko the chimp's signing. We question who and what we are. We have a sense of right and wrong.

Yet evolution is elitist, we've come to think. Animals deserve more dignity, man less. When an escaped convict in the film *Runaway Train* (Andrei Konchalovsky, 1985) is called "an animal" by a woman witnessing his cruelty, he answers: "I'm worse than an animal. I'm human" (https://www.youtube.com/watch?v=g6OI_Ia5Qdg).

The lion, we say, is the noblest of the beasts, even though the ape seems more intelligent. Both are brought back alive to serve life sentences in our zoos.

We advocate for animal rights. Animists believe that not only do lower animals have souls, but so do vegetables and rocks. The Pythagorean notion that animal souls can possess human bodies seems to explain Lear's elder daughters. Plato envisioned souls returning from heaven to a place where they chose new lives, human and animal. Human souls chose to inhabit animals, and souls of one animal species chose to inhabit another. Perhaps the Hindi notions of kharma and reincarnation (holy cows) are related to this.

In *The Naked Ape,* his 1967 bestseller, Desmond Morris revisited evolution, but from a different direction, studying our animalism in love, work, and war, and lending support to the Sexual Revolution. Thanks to sexual selection, humans have the largest penises relative to body mass. Round breasts serve as "a sexual signaling device, rather than simply for providing milk to infants." We mate to bond with each other as well as to procreate.

Stand on your dignity. Or don't. Relax.

That's beneath your dignity.

That's undignified behavior.

Civility is reasoned disagreement, dignified, rather than contemptuous or childish.

Let's discuss this like adults, we say.

Indignity. Shame. Affront. Scorn.

Self-worth, self-respect, poise.

Maintain your dignity!

Testing your dignity (protesters taunt guardsmen; God persecutes Job).

I'm too good for this. This is unbecoming.

Don't dignify that comment with a response.

How can you dignify killing with a lie? Such as war is noble?

False dignity.

Saving face, false face, face for the crowd.

My last shred of dignity.

Dignity can be forgotten, abused, wounded, lost, betrayed.

Medieval nobles were celebrated by *gisants*, sculpted likenesses on their coffin lids (Egyptian kings, also, with sarcophagi). The knight lies at rest in full armor, arms crossed over his broadsword with the cross-like hilt over his heart. On the Smith College campus, I loved Leonard Baskin's gisant of a factory worker in this traditional pose, reclining on a slab, naked, pot-bellied, care- and work-worn, aged, but noble also in his way, in our way, as if to say attention must be paid.

In "Tragedy and the Common Man" (1949), Arthur Miller argues that "the common man is as apt a subject for tragedy in its highest sense as kings were … the tragic feeling is evoked when we are in presence of a character who is ready to lay down his life, if need be, to secure one thing—his sense of personal dignity."

I love Dostoyevsky's humiliated characters.

Only humans can dehumanize themselves and each other.

Only humans, I think, project their faults and fears onto others of their kind. As in families, so in the family of man: Cain and Abel, sibling rivalries. One dignity degrades another.

We rape, we castrate, we enslave, we murder. We tyrannize. We practice genocide.

We are each other's prey and predator.

We cannibalize.

Natural enemies.

The irascible beast. Buchenwald. Jihadi John.

The Abu Ghraib torture and abuse: https://en.wikipedia.org/wiki/Abu_Ghraib_torture_and_prisoner_abuse.

Because we can.

Is dignity a right? The right to be valued? To be clothed, fed, and sheltered? To health? To birth? The right to choose?

To some, dignity seems a luxury, secondary to comfort or survival.

Are we nobler in Nature than in civilized society? Do laws and conventions, cities, conveniences, power, and governments inspire or corrupt us? For every Thoreau there is Conrad's Decoud, marooned on a desert island: "Solitude from mere outward condition of existence becomes very swiftly a state of soul in which the affectations of irony and skepticism have no place. It takes possession of the mind, and drives forth the thought into the exile of utter disbelief. After three days of waiting for the sight of some human face, Decoud caught himself entertaining a doubt of his own individuality. It had merged into the world of cloud and water, of natural forces and forms of nature.... Both his intelligence and his passion were swallowed up easily in the great unbroken solitude of waiting without faith." He shoots himself.

Can death be dignified? And for whom—the person dying, or the living who witness and endure the loss, reflecting on their own turns to come?

Cornered by life, Stoics choose suicide: "A Roman by a Roman valiantly vanquished," boasts Antony. Sudden, accidental deaths, as well as unforeseen natural ones, offend us, while death in battle, for instance, we call the greatest sacrifice.

A person with a terminal disease battles also. Cornered by their bodies, do they have a right to stop death-prolonging operations and treatments, or to opt for assisted suicide? If so, when? The moment they are diagnosed? The moment that quality of life declines? Can law and medicine offer us peace of mind, freedom from pain, and a gentle death?

"She realized that when she got right down to it, she wanted to live, more than anything, on almost any terms, so she took more cisplatin.... A month later she was off that poison ... How fast would it move, this wildfire brand? Better not to ask.... The Will to Live was more important than doctors and medicines. You had to reinvigorate the Will to Live.... Dilaudid. It wasn't working.... Was methadone the ultimate or were there bigger guns? Street heroin?" ("I Want to Live," Thom Jones).

Even those facing capital punishment can keep dignity. "Nothing in his life became him like the leaving of it," we hear of Cawdor in *Macbeth*. "He died / As one that had been studied in his death, / To throw away the dearest thing he owed / As 'twere a careless trifle."

23

Executions can be more and less humane, as well. The blindfold or hood. Axe or swordsman. Crucifixion. Hangman. Guillotine. Firing squad. Gas chamber. Electric chair. Lethal injection.

We're all on death's row, according to Elizabeth Kubler-Ross. "It is inconceivable for our unconscious to imagine an actual ending of our own life here on earth, and if this life of ours has to end, the ending is always attributed to a malicious intervention from the outside by someone else. In simple terms, in our unconscious mind, we can only be killed; it is inconceivable to die of a natural cause or of old age."

We're like Kafka's K., perhaps, baffled by etiquette: "Once more the odious courtesies began, the first handed the knife across K. to the second, who handed it across K. back again to the first. K. now perceived clearly that he was supposed to seize the knife himself, as it traveled from hand to hand above him and plunge it into his own breast. But he did not do so.... He could not completely rise to the occasion, he could not relieve the officials of all their tasks.... But the hands of one of the partners were already at K.'s throat, while the other thrust the knife deep into his heart and turned it there twice. With failing eyes K. could still see the two of them immediately before him, cheek leaning against cheeks, watching the final act. 'Like a dog,' he said; it was as if the shame of it must outlive him."

Personhood counts for everything.

Platitudes. Half-time exhortations.

What you know, you know, says Iago.

On Privilege

It's my great *privilege* to introduce. My honor/function/chance/pleasure to say publicly how I value X, and how you all should value X; to celebrate, to recommend.

Privileged information. Only a few are trusted to know; it's confidential. My Social Security number, for instance. My credit card code. Health records.

Over-privileged. Advantaged. More fortunate than necessary or deserved. Blessed. Favored. Powerful.

Under-privileged. Disadvantaged. Misfortunate. Cursed. Stigmatized. Powerless.

All men are created equal, writes the slave-owning husband and father, Thomas Jefferson, philosopher, scientist, inventor, architect, statesman, politician, patrician.

Would Darwin disagree?

What of the handsomer, brighter, more sensitive, stronger, more talented, healthier, and better coordinated among us?—these are differences by nature, rather than by choice or effort.

Still we self-improve, struggling to match gifts bestowed on others by luck.

The *privileges* of youth (an excuse for, say, poor judgment) opposed to those of age (an excuse for forgetfulness). We grant allowances.

That's her privilege, we say. We may think her tattoo was a stupid choice, but it's not for us to judge.

Entitlement. I have a right to; I deserve. (Think of Frost's "Home is the place where, when you have to go there,/ They have to take you in." "I should have called it/ Something you somehow haven't to deserve"). Still, there are privileges we earn.

Symbolic servilities. You can open the door, but here, I open it for you. I bow, I salute. I do you kindnesses. Perhaps you'll tip.

One person's privilege is another's oppression. If we had the same advantages, there would be no privilege.

Eat your greens, clean your plate, think of all the starving children in the world!

Oppressed groups agitate and demonstrate.

Oppressive laws are amended or repealed; corrective laws passed. The Thirteenth Amendment (abolished slavery), Fourteenth Amendment (guaranteed "equal protection under the laws"); the Nineteenth Amendment of 1920 (giving women the right to vote); reconstruction statutes (on Civil Action for Deprivation of Rights, Conspiracies to Interfere with Civil Rights, Deprivation of Rights Under Color of Law, Peonage Abolished); the Civil Rights Act of 1964, forbidding discrimination based on "race, color, religion, or national origin" in public establishments; Title IX of Education Amendments of 1972 forbidding exclusion from or discrimination under any education program or activity receiving Federal financial assistance; the proposed Equal Rights Amendment, that all rights under the Constitution "apply equally to all persons regardless of their sex" of 1972-82 (never passed, but still in dispute).

Slogans are chanted. Myths and icons challenged. Pronouns changed.

Male and white, straight, employed and able-bodied, I should mind my manners, consider others, and reexamine my attitudes towards "difference." I think I've got it. I'm a fair man, a good man. An earnest citizen. I fancy myself fair-minded.

I need to re-examine my place in oppression: that men have been privileged over women, whites over people of color, straights over LGBTs, rich over poor, management over labor, marrieds over singles, Christians over other believers (and unbelievers), Protestants over Catholics, Presbyterians over Baptists, slender bodies over heavy.

Homophobia, for instance, is fear of the feminine within. We scapegoat where we doubt.

Prejudice is a sickness of privilege, afflicting both the host and victim.

We owe each other due regard.

Willingly, responsibly, I learn to listen.

*

And yet, what of reverse discrimination? Reparations? Affirmative action? I feel oppressed (writ small) as I am categorized by gender, race, and age, and disregarded as an individual. My worth is contested, complexity dismissed. Payback, I admit. Where society privileges, it can also penalize.

*

Take literature, for another instance, my vocation. Here is Terry Eagleton: "There is no such thing as a literary work or tradition which is valuable in itself.... 'Value' is a transitive term: it means whatever is valued by certain people in specific situations, according to particular criteria and in light of given purposes." Accordingly, the Western Canon is dismissed as works by Dead White European Males, which perpetuates patriarchal, capitalist, and racist values. Forget the beauty, glory, and imaginative capacity of such works, since they've failed to celebrate or *failed to be celebrated* for granting "agency" to women, the proletariat, or people of color. Imagination itself, then, appears to be only a projection of cultural experience rather than of essential humanity. Harold Bloom protests against such ideas: "to connect the study of literature with the quest for social change [is a mistake]," he argues. "Without the [Western] Canon, we cease to think. Either there were aesthetic values, or there are only the over-determinations of race, class, and gender. You must choose." Still, Toni Morrison's *Playing In The Dark* illuminates Hemingway, allowing both for aesthetics and racial coding: "A criticism that needs to insist that literature is not only 'universal' but also 'race-free' risks lobotomizing that literature, and diminishes both the art and the artist." And Morrison's reading of American classics seems congruent with Bloom's reading of *The Merchant of Venice* in *Shakespeare And The Invention Of The Human.* When my daughter graduated from Hampshire College in 1997, she had read none of Bloom's Canon, a lapse I still regret for her; but she has dedicated her life to social justice and principles of non-violence, to writing, painting, and teaching, and to parenting, and her chosen library is as present to her (and strange to me) as mine is to me and strange to her.

From my library, Albert Camus writes: "Those who find no rest in God or in history are condemned to live for those who, like themselves, cannot live: in fact, for the humiliated" (*The Rebel,* 1951). His solidarity in the absurd, partly Marxist, partly a response to the Holocaust, recalls the once-privileged Lear's remonstrance to privilege: "Take Physic, Pomp, / Expose thyself to feel what wretches feel / That thou mayst shake the superflux to them / And show the heavens more just." Of course, Count Leo Tolstoy, giving up his property late in life and dressing like a peasant, seems cranky and affected, while the redistribution of wealth under Communism privileged bureaucrats, commissars, and Stalin.

*

Sexual harassment, we are told by human resources officials, is as oppressive as racial discrimination. If it is or was the way of the world, like bribery and greed, it is a wrong way. And rather than our being tough enough to endure it, we should be tough on it. Call it out. Take it to court, if necessary. Power disparity negates mutual consent.

At first, in the 1990s, I had trouble identifying with harassment concerns. I respected boundaries, yes. But what of friendship in the workplace, between supervisor and worker, professor and assistant professor, teacher and student? Was it fraternizing, in the military sense? Did it distract from professionalism? Did it privilege a promotion or a grade, or appear to? Where was the allowance for humor, affinity, comradery or proportion? A desk photo of a wife in a bikini was inappropriate. A closed office door with a student invited suspicion. Later, I understood, having been routinely cornered by a department chairman and forced to listen to his fantasies of success with his novels; or having my college president direct me to flatter a wealthy donor, who then bothered me with calls to my home. I squirmed in these situations and despised my self-betrayal.

Objectification is related to harassment. I check my gaze. I struggle with the beauty myth, who's hot, and who's not, and why, and for whom. Women judge women, too, viewing through their idea of male eyes. Perhaps no difference is more prone to fantasy and self-hatred, as any teenager knows. Glamor is privileged over essence. Other attractions, such as character and personality, follow on looks. While fashion, cosmetics, hair dye, Jenny Craig, and surgical improvements offer to correct our flawed natures, for a price, most of us are not for all markets. Might we all fare better, I wonder, if nudity were taken for granted or if we all wore togas, muumuus or Maoist pajamas?

*

Consider the Boston Marathon, the only marathon where dedicated runners of different nations, ethnicities, genders, and capacities must qualify by making stringent times for their age groups in another marathon. Differences are allowed for, focusing on achievement according to factors of luck and physical givens. Men are physically larger and stronger than women. The young are physically stronger and more flexible than the old. Runners with legs are privileged over those in wheelchairs. Each competitive group has its starting time. First, the women's, then the men's wheelchair athletes. Then the elite women runners, expected to finish in 2:20 to 3:00 hours. Then the elite men, expected to finish in 2:08 to 2:45 hours. Then the runners of both sexes grouped by slower qualifying times, expected to finish in four hours, although those running for various sponsors and charities may take six or more. The idea is to distribute the 20,000 some runners along the narrow course, and to keep them out of each other's way. There are champions and placers for each group, except for the non-competitive back of the pack, where finishing is its own achievement. All finishers get medals, jackets, and Mylar capes. Though the field is overwhelmingly American and white, since 1988 only three non-Africans have won the men's race. The Kenyans and Ethiopians are particularly gifted with lean, small bodies, but they are also culturally driven, selected young and state-supported. Running becomes their way out from poverty, and when they win, they reinvest the prize money back home.

*

There are lucky lives, no question. But even the luckiest is visited with suffering, and even the most wretched with measures of joy. I believe that. The long haul is more leveling than we admit. The distribution more just. Or is this only a belief? All is vanity, sayeth the Preacher. "Call no man fortunate that is not dead" (Yeats), Oedipus's example suggests. Privilege is the chance to fail.

*

In James Alan McPherson's 1968 story, "Gold Coast," James Sullivan, the elderly Irish janitor for a Cambridge apartment building assumes power over Robert, the narrator, who is black, young, and a writer with potential. Robert works as the janitor's apprentice. For Robert, it is a temporary job and source of material, while for Sullivan it is a closed destiny under both owners and tenants. Sullivan patronizes his apprentice and advises him on his station; he also offers friendship, intruding on Robert's privacy. Robert indulges Sullivan, listens to his bigotry, and feels sufficient in his talents, youth, record collection, and white girlfriend. However, his sufficiency is undermined when "social forces" cause him to lose the girlfriend and for a while he bonds with Sullivan ("having him there was much better than being alone"). Then as Robert's youth reasserts itself, Sullivan's misery becomes too oppressive to tolerate ("I did not want to hear any more and he would know he was making a burden of himself"). Robert moves on, leaving Sullivan behind him. Having witnessed, he will tell Sullivan's story and his own, but privilege demands self-preservation.

*

Supposedly, the privileged became monks in the Middle Ages and most failed to reproduce. In the Russian Revolution, comrades slaughtered the aristocrats. The Third Reich practiced unnatural selection, resulting in devolution. ISIS seems fixed on a similar goal.

G.I. Jane. Women in combat and policing. Contrary to being saved first, now women may stand, if they wish, in harm's way.

I wonder in our idealism, are we over-sensitive? Too thin-skinned and fastidious? Is it a fault of the over-privileged to think so?

Recognize your janitor, I am reminded, because my custom has been to take him or her for granted, as if she or he were invisible. Every job has dignity.

*

Captain Miller (Tom Hanks) to Private Ryan (Matt Dillon) at the end of the film *Saving Private Ryan:* "Earn this. Earn it." As a survivor, Ryan's duty is to make his life worth the sacrifices of other soldiers, who have died to save it.

31

A privileged narrator knows her or his characters' fates, feelings, and thoughts. Usually, he or she shares these with the reader, creating narrative irony. We know more than the characters in their errors and we pity and sympathize with their limited awareness or perspective both about themselves and about others. Think of Oedipus's unwitting killing of his father. My favorite moments are when the characters then discover the truth too late, and rise to some self-affirming action (Oedipus's self-blinding, Othello's suicide), where they seem to know more than we do.

Aesthetic distance, of course, where readers have no chance to intervene, is different from social distance, where in fact and in spirit, in small acts and large, we can reject oppression and take our place in a braver, more generous world.

Life is our privilege. Every breath we take.

On Dreams

Besides good and bad dreams, there are different categories.

There is the conscious dream of ambition, a driving goal or ideal, often over practical objections. *It was, has been, is my dream to write and publish work that lasts.* We also dream for our children and others in that sense. Take George Willard's mother in Sherwood Anderson's *Winesburg, Ohio:* "He is not a dull clod, all words and smartness. Within him there is a secret something that is striving to grow. It is the thing I let be killed in myself."

Another kind is "precognitive" or unconscious, a mental experience while we sleep, whether we remember it or not when we wake. *I dreamt that I could fly.* In that sense, we're said to dream nightly.

Yet another kind is a sacred message delivered in trance or sleep, such as the prophetic dreams reported in the Bible: *God came to Noah in a dream.*

We also daydream, choosing our dreams like Walter Mitty. We fantasize about our magical bravery, success, luck, irresistibility, brilliance, etc., while consciously despairing of ourselves.

We share the dreams of art, expressing our visions about the nature and meaning of things. Lily Briscoe, the painter at the end of Virginia Woolf's *To The Lighthouse,* thinks, "*I have had my vision.*"

As an adjective, dream means the best conceivable, such as my dream car, dream lover, dream job, dream dream.

Dreams that we mistake for reality, we call hallucinations: the giant proves windmill, the dagger before us can't be grasped, the water we thirst for vanishes on approach.

Pipe dreams are hallucinations under one chemical influence or another.

We have collective dreams as well, such as our American Dream; political dreams ("A chicken in every pot"); and conditioned dreams, thanks to advertising and brainwashing.

Since animals dream, too—the sleeping dog, twitching and scrabbling its paws, as if chasing prey—not all dreams are verbal or rational. A poet friend, Thomas Lux, started The Barn Dream Press, named for what cows might dream as they return from pasture.

You should honor your dreams, sleep experts say. Write them down on waking. Tell them to someone. Think about them as coded messages. Look for puns and symbols. Recall them while you can. I'm trying to express something that my dream mind knows but my waking mind resists. That's therapy's idea, anyhow.

Here's one that's haunted me. When I was 27—at the height of the Vietnam War protests, the Beatles, Woodstock, and drug and sex experimentation—I dreamed that I was unlocking my car near a solemn building where a party had been. My older doctor brother, Charles, appeared and needed me to drive him to his waiting car. We two got in. As I backed out, a hot-rod full of young, drunken kids (I was drunk too, I realized) came pushing at me, honking, with its headlights and jeering faces. They wanted me out of the way, but gave me no room to turn. I was in the narrow passage to the highway, then, a busy, no-nonsense highway, but deserted now, and they kept butting my front bumper. We realized that it was futile to resist, so I backed onto the highway, engine whining, hoping to get out of their way. Still they forced me down the highway in reverse until I had to pull over no matter what, but knew if slowed down, they would smash into me. I turned my lights on and off and blinked high and low beams as a warning. Finally, I touched my brakes and began to back off to the side, only to glimpse them coming and swerving past.

My right front fender hit their left rear, on which, clinging hilariously, was one of the kids. A loud crunch and the kid mashed, like pictures of the bullet shattering Kennedy's head: sudden, irremediable. They pulled ahead and stopped across the road, while I stopped on the shoulder, facing away, and trembling. My brother fumed: "Look what you've done! Jesus, I thought you were handling them, but then you pull a dumb stunt!" I wanted to make it up. "You're a doctor," I said. "Can't you go help?" "The kid's dead," he said. He didn't even want to try. We started up and sped off in search of the police—around a corner into a lighted, but deserted town. I rehearsed my statement for the cops. I had to hide being drunk. Also that I'd failed to signal with my blinker. I hadn't slowed down slowly enough; I'd touched the brakes too soon. Charles accused me of losing my temper and not using my head. I imagined the outraged, detailed inquiries from the boy's parents. How was this valuable life lost? "You did that just to save your face!" Charles said.

Yes, Dr. Freud, it's about sibling rivalry, among other things. Ego against Id. My failed self-control harming others, or the "other" in myself. Winners and wasters. Life styles/impulses colliding. The threat of regression. For $30, I could have it interpreted here: http://www.dreamresearch.ca/services.php.

Richard Ford says that other persons' dreams are self-absorbed and boring to strangers. "I try to ignore dreams. I can't think of any reason I should tell a dream to anybody that could be anything more to someone else than watching cartoons ... dreams to me, mean selfish gestures" (*Writers Dreaming*, ed. Naomi Epel, Vintage, 1983).

The literature of Europe's Late Middle Ages was big on Dream Visions as a form, from *Piers Plowman* to the *Romance of the Rose* to *The Divine Comedy* to *Pilgrim's Progress*. The dreams were moral allegories.

Shakespeare foregrounds his debunkers of dreams, for the most part soldiers, skeptics, cynics, materialists and practical worldlings.

Mercutio: "I see Queen Mab has been with you." Theseus: "The poet, the madman, and the lover are of imagination all compact." Cleopatra to Dolabella: "You laugh when boys or women tell their dreams; / Is't not your trick?" In the dreams that are his plays, sceptics prove wrong, of course. Romeo's premonition of his fate comes true, though Mercutio dismisses it as "nothing"; as does, perhaps, Romeo's dream later of "reviving' with his lady's kiss to be an Emperor. Thanks to Oberon and Puck, the young males in *Midsummer* do swap beloveds, causing their beloveds to blame each other; and Bottom transformed to a literal ass becomes the paramour of the Fairy Queen. But only Bottom, referring to 1 Corinthians 2:9-10, realizes that his dream was true: "I have had a most rare vision. I have had a dream, past the wit of man to say what dream it was." In a much later play, Dolabella's doubts are countered by Cleopatra's vision of Antony and lost in her retort: "It's past the size of dreaming. Nature wants stuff / To vie strange forms with fancy; yet t'imagine / An Antony were Nature's piece 'gainst fancy, / Condemning shadows quite."

Today's dream researchers would have made Mercutio, Theseus, and Dolabella proud. "One prominent neurobiological theory of dreaming is the 'activation-synthesis hypothesis,' which states that dreams don't actually mean anything: they are merely electrical brain impulses that pull random thoughts and imagery from our memories" (Sandor van der Linden in *The Scientific American,* http://www.scientificamerican. com/article/the-science-behind-dreaming/). Subjects are wired and left to sleep, while researchers monitor their brave waves. Their most "vivid" dreams take place during so-called Rapid Eye Movement sleep and register as impulses on the researchers' instruments. In addition to REM dreaming, they've discovered that we may dream four or more times a night during non-REM sleep. The non-REM phase seems to produce fragmented memories, while the REM phase connects and applies these memories towards dealing with the future. Dreams, in this sense, can help subjects to perform better at on-going tasks. "Sleep on it," is familiar advice, when we're faced with impasses and challenges. "The dreams that we have during REM sleep, they're very wild.

They're very fanciful. They're clearly the brain having a period of loose associations, where you are able to put connections together, between new and old ideas, finding new solutions to new problems," states Sara Mednick on PBS Nova's 'What Are Dreams?' (http://www.pbs.org/wgbh/nova/body/what-are-dreams.html). Since other mammals dream as well, the activity may be an ancient defense mechanism, whereby simulating threats, our brains train for response and escape. Advocates of "threat simulation theory" think the dream function contributes to our survival, our creativity, and our problem solving abilities, but still regard the dreams themselves as mostly nonsense. "It was only a dream," we tell our children, hoping to comfort them.

Eloise, the suburban housewife in J. D. Salinger's "Uncle Wiggly in Connecticut," having lost her true love in WW2, finds herself trapped in a materialistic marriage and destroys her daughter's imaginary friend with violent realism: "Eloise grabbed Ramona's ankles and half lifted and half pulled her over to the middle of the bed."

My wife made a papier-mâché *baku*, a "dream-eater," for the progressive elementary school where she taught. What a great concept, I thought. According to Chinese and Japanese folklore, the *baku* was created by the gods from parts left over from making other animals. My wife's had a bear's body, elephant's trunk and mouth, rhinoceros's eyes, tigers's feet, and an oxen tail, all painted garish yellows, reds, greens, whites and blues. The size of a big dog, open-mouthed with serrated teeth and hollow inside, her *baku* stood on a table outside of the principal's office. Kids wrote down their nightmares and fed them into its mouth, and then, supposedly, each dream's power was devoured. Secretly, the teachers read the dreams, but stopped when the kids' parents started leaving serious, twisted dreams of their own, as if the *baku* were a reverse wishing well or confession booth.

Her classes also made "dreamcatchers." Following Native American traditions, these looked like badminton rackets. Webs of colored yarn were woven over willow hoops and decorated with beads and feathers.

Hung over your bed, the dreamcatcher supposedly protected you from nightmares. Only good dreams could filter through. The dreams originated, supposedly, from good and evil spirits surrounding the sleeper.

Most of my dreams fail to interest even me, let alone others. Most are like bad writing: shallow, weakly imagined, and rambling; a form of mental chatter. In so-called lucid dreaming, however, when half-awake, I can direct or coax my dreams and improve them as I go.

"Dreams are the ordinary person's art," suggests Reynolds Price (Epel, op. cit.). "I mean people who don't write poetry, etc., do in fact, every night when they're asleep, construct works of art in their heads." And Robert Stone, speaking as a novelist, admits that "the same thing that's going on in my work is often going on in my dreams" (Epel).

John Sayles, both novelist and filmmaker, loses himself in a form of lucid dreaming. "One of the reasons I like to swim is that I get good ideas then. Or when I'm running. With that physical activity and lack of other input, I can put myself into a trance. I fall into a state that's not totally conscious fairly easily" (Epel).

On a long run once, I experienced such a state, which bordered on hallucination. I clearly heard the voices of my dead, my mother, father, two older brothers, and nephew, congratulating and encouraging me, not just in running, but in my life. Their voices felt as close and real as the day and landscape itself, and left me feeling buoyed and gladdened.

When I do have a memorable dream, the emotions are what matters. In retelling it, I try to recreate the dreamer as a character, and if necessary to sharpen or invent details that will lead the reader to feel as the dreamer feels. In "Forces of Nature: A Dream Retold," from *Safe Suicide* (2008), my dreamer is on a trip away from his family, when he hears that their friends have lost their birth son to cancer.

His own son has been adopted as an infant from Korea. That night, he dreams that some sort of flood spares his family, while sweeping away the children of Korean refugees. The refugees surround him and clamor for his son's return. Unable to reason with them, he wakes: "to my life where there is no ... catastrophe. But where there is guilt, always. And where I will never, ever, take the blessing of my son for granted."

Hollywood, "the dream factory," tries with visual and aural narrative to rival our dream mind and emotions. One of my favorite films, the 1939 *King Kong*, seems almost pedantic in its dream imagery. Caves. Water. Repeated images of falling. All sorts of phallic imagery framed by the fear of rape and forbidden love. Images of size and power. My wife and I forbade our young son to view it on TV for fear it would give him nightmares.

In a different sense, John Gardner in *On Moral Fiction,* claims that fiction is "a vivid and continuous dream," which appeals to our senses. In bad writing, he argues, "some mistake or conscious ploy on the part of the artist" interrupts the dream and forces us "to think of the writer or writing." He also poses the power of serious art to move, teach, and transport us, while grounding us in self-awareness.

In dreams begin responsibilities.

In college, I made up a dream to freak out my roommate, a psych major, who slept in the bunk below. I told him a snake had emerged from my anus, coiled down the bedframe and strangled him in his sleep. "Hey, hey, no, I'm only joking," I promised. "Relax." He wouldn't believe me.

Frank Conroy laughed at Freudian readings of his autobiography, *Stop-time.* "There's a scene when my mother is sitting on the toilet as she tells me my father is dead, then flushes. Nothing could be more 'Freudian' than that," he said. "But it's what *happened.*"

The naïve and sheltered are surprised by undreamt of cruelties and grief, the tidal wave, the plague; while the sophisticated and exposed are surprised by kindness and joy, the lost love found, the second chance, forgiveness and redemption. Beyond our wildest dreams, we say.

We're not in Kansas anymore.

Curiouser and curiouser, thinks Alice.

Row, row, row your boat.

Beautiful dreamer, wake unto me.

She still beheld / Now wide awake, the vision of her sleep.

I see the promised land.

On Cursing

Cartoons offer a cat, pig, duck, or wolf with an enraged face, said figure having hit its hoof, paw, or wing with a hammer, and its dialogue balloon reads: "#!@#&*!!"

"Cushlamachree!" is the cigar-smoking, fairy godfather's handy expletive in Crockett Johnson's WW2 cartoon epic, *Barnaby* (published before Johnson's *Harold and The Purple Crayon*). You may recall other substitutes for swearing from early and mid-century popular culture such as: Aw, gosh darn! Heck. Drat. Nuts. Gol-darn, anyway. Phooey. That stinks. Ouch! Damnation! Dag-nabit! Alas! Curses! Darn it. Crud. Screw off. What a revolting development. Good grief! Geewilikers! Ay, caramba! Go to blazes! Suffering succotash!

"*For Whom The Bell Tolls* is foul-mouthed," observes Se Think (https://sethink.wordpress.com/2011/04/19/sex-swearing-and-other-transliterations-in-ernest-hemingways-for-whom-the-bell-tolls/). "Not explicitly so, because the novel would have never been read in its day if Hemingway had not censored himself. But he substitutes the words 'obscenity' or 'unprintable' in ways that leave the intended word clear. Or he uses a word that rhymes with the intended word. In a moment of frustration, a character rants beautifully for most of a page with a 'Oh, muck my grandfather and muck this whole treacherous muck-faced mucking country and every mucking Spaniard in it on either side and to hell forever. Muck them to hell together....'" Maxwell Perkins, Hemingway's editor, pressured him to "emasculate his prose" (however, Hemingway did at last spell out "fuck" in 1937's *To Have and Have Not*).

Fear of censorship probably begins with #3 of the Ten Commandments: "You shall not take the name of the LORD your God in vain." Observant Jews avoid spelling out "G-d."

Curses are different from cusses or swears, though they often merge. A curse calls down evil on someone, circumstance, or thing: "God damn you/it!" A swear is an insult, comparing someone or thing to an animal in regard to stupidity, loveless sex, and lack of spirit or reason, or to a body part or product (usually from the reproductive or excretory systems); or to a socially despised, feared, or "different" group (in race, nationality, class, gender, hygiene, and/or sexual preferences and acts). We speak of "dirty" words, as related to poor toilet training ("potty mouth"), or to the poverty of "unwashed millions." We need such words to project the aspects we hate or think we should hate about ourselves. Also, we often use stock swear words as exclamations of pain, shock, or frustration. Shit and fuck seem interchangeable with, say, Sweet Jesus, the profane with the sacred.

We (well-bred, estimable, moral, and polite members of society) designate a certain lexicon of words, comparisons, and gestures to be: profane (as opposed to reverent), obscene (as opposed to decent), offensive (as opposed to pleasant), coarse (as opposed to refined), earthy (as opposed to heavenly), explicit (as opposed to implicit or guarded), shocking (as opposed to calming), strong (as opposed to weak or diluted), salty (as opposed to land-based), foul (as opposed to fair or tasteful), colorful (as opposed to bland), indecent (as opposed to decent), gutter/street (as opposed to hearth or parlor), bad (as opposed to good), dirty (as opposed to clean), vulgar/crude (as opposed to refined), common (as opposed to noble), low (as opposed to high), raw (as opposed to cooked and easy to digest).

As early language learners, we're told such words are forbidden (at least to children) and are punished for using them, despite our hearing them on TV and from older children and other adults; then as adults, we tell our own children the same, and this is reinforced as they are supervised in school (if not on playgrounds or the street). As they're called names, we tell them, "Sticks and stones may break your bones, but names will never hurt you." When they are angry, instead of hitting, we tell them to "use your words." However, if they should swear or call names, we warn them to watch their language and threaten to wash their mouths out with soap.

See Jamaica Kinkaid's *New Yorker* story "Girl," where the colonialized mother insists on good language and manners that will help her daughter get ahead: "don't sing benna in Sunday school; you mustn't speak to wharf-rat boys...." Or think of *My Fair Lady*, where Eliza is trained by Henry Higgins to drop her Cockney vernacular and speak proper English.

My executive father's only curse was "damn," although that, so infrequent, and so vehement, shocked and frightened us. My mother, my two older brothers, my sister, and I never went even that far at home, at least not out loud, at least not to my memory. Thinking I was alone once at age 8 or 9, working in my improvised darkroom in our basement, when I spilled developer on an open package of printing paper, I shouted: FUCK, SHIT, HELL, DAMN! I wasn't alone, however. My sister had come down for laundry and appeared suddenly in my doorway. *Dee! Dee, was that you? I can't believe I'd ever hear those words out of your mouth. I won't tell, but you know better than that.*

Swearing, like wielding swords or guns, was by convention (Puritan? Victorian? Patriarchal?), a privilege of men in adult male company, but was forbidden in the presence of women or children. Men of my father's age and station swore openly as they padded around in towels and sandals in the golf club locker room. And a man who didn't swear was thought unmanly. Of course, when I caddied for hire on ladies' day and was treated as invisible and utilitarian, I learned that women swore as well.

I love swearing women, such as Eudora Welty's old maid Clytie, in the story of the same name, who would go into the family garden and have swearing fits: "The cursing was new, and she cursed softly, like a singer going over a song for the first time. But it was something she could not stop. Words which at first horrified Clytie poured in a full, light stream from her throat, which soon, nevertheless, felt strangely relaxed and rested. She cursed all alone in the peace of the vegetable garden. Everybody said, in something like deprecation, that she was only imitating her older sister, who used to go out to that same garden and curse in the same way, years ago, but in a remarkably loud, commanding voice that could be heard in the post office."

And then there's the deranged Ophelia, suddenly as bawdy as if she has been to a nunnery (the Elizabethan pun for whore house). Her license is madness: "Young men will do do't if they come to't: / By Cock, they are to blame." Involuntary bawdry is an example of what psychiatry calls coprolalia: "utterance of obscene words or socially inappropriate and derogatory remarks." From the Greek, the word means "to talk of feces."

*

Think of how much cursing invokes our unexamined, juvenile anxieties: body image, status, homosexuality, incest, masturbation, and defecation; and how imaginatively limited our common curses are. Our small store of "profane" words and ideas seems archaic, working as verbal reflexes or gestures, rather than as intentional metaphors. We call someone an asshole, for instance, a jerk, a shithead, a slob, a motherfucker, a bastard, a bitch. Socially and psychologically, we need such insults to assert our superiority, implying that we are none of these things, but rather we are group-approved, normal, savvy, a brain or heart, a heterosexual lover, a legitimate family member, a good (and probably male) dog. Hand gestures can reinforce or stand in for the spoken curse, most commonly the middle finger for *up yours* or *fuck you*. For the complete lexicon, see: http://www.noswearing.com/ dictionary/ and http://www.slate.com/blogs/lexicon_valley/2013/09/ 11/top_swear_words_most_popular_curse_words_on_facebook. html. Also: https://www.indy100.com/article/british-swear-words-ranked-ofcom-7340446.

As for the actual body parts and functions, turn to TV's Dr. Ruth. Society approves the medical words for those: vagina, vulva, labia, clitoris, penis, scrotum, testicles, anus, gluteus maximus, mammary glands, sexual intercourse, oral sex, fellatio/cunnilingus, etc.; terms supposedly "colorless" and without emotional charge. Of course, in some cultures or subcultures—the military, for instance, teen gangs, work crews, pop music bands, prison, barrooms and poorer neighborhoods (note the swear jar in Luke Cage's barber shop in the recent Marvel/Netflix series)—clinical words probably seem more disturbing than profane ones. "People who have grown up in environments without language control often do not understand the very concept of good language and bad language. They seem to wonder at the hang-ups of those people who do not use foul language," writes David Yeagley. "Foul mouth people seem to feel superior to the neurotic types who act so offended when bad words are used. Law and political correctness, in a desperate media environment, are not enough to explain why there is such a thing as foul language and pure language." (From an article on BadEagle. com, since removed.)

At least in the secularized West, we've moved beyond the "Civilization and Its Discontents" of Freud's day. Literature, film and TV have defeated the last vestiges of censorship and mass market propriety. The "standards of decency" that in the 1960s determined ratings of G, PG, R, and X have pretty much been leveled to R. Graphic images of sex, full-frontal nudity, and violence now accompany and illustrate the swear words, leaving nothing, as they say, to imagination. Think of Howard Stern, shock jock; of Denis Leary's stand-up monologues; of David Milch's dialogue in the HBO series *Deadwood,* all of which seemed brazen at first, but now seem normative. A certain equation of realism, expose, and psychological hygiene has won out. We're sophisticated. Let's drop the pretense and hypocrisy. Let's be adult. Get real. Say it like it is. There's solidarity in common denominators. Or perhaps, in line with Orwell's idea of "Politics and the English Language," we think our nitty-gritty guards against deception by euphemism. Curse for authenticity. Curse for protest. Just as we wear pricy sneakers and faded jeans to fancy occasions instead of formal wear: clothes don't make the man or power. While we stand for social and political justice, informal has become our formal.

"Swearing is like using the horn on your car, which can be used to signify a number of emotions (e.g., anger, frustration, joy, surprise)," writes the swearing expert, Professor Timothy Jay of Massachusetts College of Liberal Arts. But once we're desensitized to the cursing lexicon, and to the shame, prejudices, and taboos that once gave it power, we become horn-deaf. Technology can compensate, amplifying volume and magnifying scale instead of meaning, but it's time for an overhaul. Our curses need more art, imagination and wit, I think, to recover energy. And for that to happen, we need to revisit our deepest vulnerabilities. We need wildness. We need vision.

The flytings or cursing contests of Falstaff (old, fat) and Prince Hal (young, thin) perpetually delight us. Thrust—"PRINCE: These lies are like their father who begets them, gross as a mountain, open, palpable. Why, thou clay-brained guts, thou knotty-pated fool, thou whoreson obscene greasy tallow-catch …"—is met by counter-thrust—"FALSTAFF: 'Sbood, you starvling, you eel-skin, you dried neats-tongue, you bull's pizzle, you stockfish—O for breath to utter what is like thee!—you tailor's yard, you sheath, you bowcase, you vile standing tuck!"

Perhaps, as some suggest, rap and hip hop have this kind of energy, abetted by the angry beat, stabbing rhymes, and hand gestures. A study of "Profanity in Popular Rap Music (1985-2013)" counts 31,564 instances of cuss words in 145 albums. Words counted include "Fuck, Shit, Bitch, Pussy, Ho, N-Words, Dick, Cock, Homophobic Slurs, G-Damn, Skeet, Tits, Cunt, Ass." Tupac's album "All Eyez on Me" alone has 905 instances (http://www.shortlist.com/entertainment/music/statistical-history-of-swearing-in-rap).

But for my money, the most powerful cursing in our language is the powerless King Lear's. He doesn't yell in our idiom: You lying bitch! You shit-eating, two-faced cunt! Fuck you! (compare Edward Albee's *Who's Afraid of Virginia Woolf*). Instead, infantilized by his treacherous eldest daughter, Goneril, he strikes out at the basics of reproduction:

> Hear, Nature, hear; dear Goddess, hear:
> Suspend thy purpose if thou didst intend
> To make this creature fruitful.
> Into her womb convey sterility,
> Dry up her organs of increase,
> And from her derogate body never spring
> A babe to honor her.

This goes beyond anxiety into the realm of our profoundest taboos: as a daughter disowns her father, a father wants to deny his daughter the ability to have children: unnatural indeed. Her organs of increase? Her ovaries! Her father curses her ovaries! He calls for her sterility. Then later calls again for something like the plague or bone cancer: "Strike her young bones, /You taking airs, with lameness." He wants her afflicted, as he feels afflicted. He calls on lightning to blind her and on "fen-sucked fogs" to "infect her beauty … blister her pride." Finally he calls for global catastrophe: "Strike flat the thick rotundity of the world, / Crack Nature's molds, all germains spill at once / That makes ingrateful man!" Demolish the planet, demolish our sperm, eggs, our DNA, our very species. This is unthinkable, let alone unmentionable. It dares damnation, as it were. It puts the grotesque horrors of Senecan melodrama and sensationalism to shame, as it does the grotesqueries of our horror films.

Perhaps only the greatest of literary tragedies register the outer limits of the sacred and profane. Words fail Lear at the unforeseen worst, the loss of his only faithful, capacious, loving and beloved daughter, Cordelia, a loss in which he himself is both victim and to blame. His world-annihilating curses are reduced to the raw, drawn-out animal cry of "Howl, howl, howl, howl!" We see it in the Holocaust. We see it on the evening news, the pieta videos of atrocity, of bomb-torn children, cradled in their wailing parents' arms. "Look there, look there."

*

Ah, fuck! Enough. My only conclusion is Cole Porter's 1934 lyric: "Good authors too / who once knew better words / Now only use four-letter words … / writing prose, anything goes."

On Voice

I'd never seen or imagined vocal cords. Heard about them, of course—the voice box, the larynx. The word "cords" suggests string instruments, where a finger pluck or felt hammer causes vibrations at different frequencies, high notes, middle, and low. But here I'm about to have a medical procedure where the Ear, Nose and Throat doctor, having first anesthetized my throat, so there will be no gag reflex, slides down a tiny camera on a wire. The relaxing spray stings at first, but not badly, and tastes tart like pineapple. There is a video console on a cart next to my examination chair. She asks me to lean forward, my mouth wide, and works the camera down inside me. She tells me to swallow; to say AAAAA, to say EEEEE. I do my best, although the wire in my throat feels in the way, and hard.

In the replay of my exam, I see a glistening pink cavern, reminiscent of my colonoscopy video. I don't see any cords, so much as lumps of muscle. As the muscles clench and relax, they are attached to thin membranes, like wings, and the membrane edges have a thick, whitish fold. As the folds part they reveal a dark opening. The doctor points and touches the screen. The thickened folds, like lips, are the so-called cords. Air, pushed out by my lungs and diaphragm, causes them to vibrate. My problem, she explains, one common at my age, is that my cords can't close all the way. I see that. The rims have bowed outwards. Humming in different tones causes the membranes to open and close, like curtains. For my EEEEE sound, the curtains should close, but a remaining gap lets air escape. Hence my wavering and breathiness. Voice exercises will help, the doctor says, especially as I learn to work with vibrations in the mouth and lips. Another remedy would be Teflon injections, which puff up the vocal muscles and force the cords to meet; but this lasts only for three to six months. The condition itself can't be fixed. I opt for the exercises, at least for now. I don't need my voice to project or have normal clarity, since I've retired from teaching.

*

Only mammals have a larynx, which controls air pressure to the vocal cords, and hence volume. Dog's bark, cat's meow, cow's moo, horse's whinny, whale's moan. Instead of a larynx, birds have a bony structure called a syrinx at the bottom of the windpipe. It is surrounded by an air sac, filled from both lungs, and allows them to warble, trill, chirp, cluck, squawk, cry and shriek. Parrots and parakeets, thanks to their thick tongues, curved beaks, long windpipes, specialized sets of neck muscles, and keen hearing, manage to imitate the complex sounds of human speech: "Polly wants a cracker!" In snakes, air fills an organ called the glottis, then when forced out, causes parts within the glottis to rattle, which produces the hissing sound.

*

What is it about voices? We recognize those of intimate others in the dark, or on the phone, whether near or far away. The first spoken syllable, its timbre, is as familiar as the speaker. "Hey, it's me," we say. Friend, family, lover, no one needs to say their names. Sometimes when I have a bad cold, though, my voice drops a register, causing friends to ask is that me? "That doesn't sound like you," they say. Electronic instruments can recognize voice prints, which like fingerprints, are unique. Given a known voice sample, the squiggly graph on the audio file can identify me, or out of the babble of cell phone surveillance, Pablo Escobar.

*

I listen to my daughter's voice, which I taped thirty years ago, and play back now for her daughters, aged 13 and 7. Ruth had been born the year my father died. My mother lived alone in their four-bedroom ranch in Villanova, PA; and my tape was from our visit from Boston. Ruth was three, boosted by phonebooks in her chair, with me beside her, Connie across and Mom at the head of the formal, mahogany dining table, chandelier fixture overhead. Mom had served us a stew. I cut small pieces of sausage on Ruth's plate and added a spot of ketchup. She ate the carrots, potatoes, celery and peas with her fork, but wasn't interested in the remaining slivers of sausage. I tried to make a game of cutting a sliver of my own, then spearing and holding it in front of my mouth as an example. "Hey, meat!" I said. "Hello, Mr. Meat. Goodbye, Meat," and chomped it from my fork. My mother's voice, meanwhile, is in the background, along with Connie's. They're discussing our return to Boston the next morning. Next, spearing a piece from Ruth's plate, I held it in front of her. "Hey, Meat!" she sang in that ascending, high-pitched trill of hers. "Hi, Meat!" But she wouldn't bite.

Even after decades, daughter with daughters now, mother long since passed, there is the shock of recognition in forgotten rhythms and timbres. I listen and go on later to imagine the other voices I know. Voices of my older brothers. My father. Close friends. I'm ready to hear and recognize them, though I haven't heard them alive for decades. Some living voices, however, I can't summon. The voices of schoolmates at our 50th reunion, for instance, have no print in memory. They could call, as two did afterwards, "Hey, know who this is?" I didn't. Their breaths against their vocal cords.

My brother, Jack, having quit college, visited home when I was 10, with Lady, part collie, part something else, a dog that he had rescued from abuse in a Colorado logging camp. He left her with us as he returned to Colorado, and I became her surrogate master. From time to time, he called long-distance. I held the phone to Lady's ear; Jack spoke and gave his special whistle, driving her beserk with joy, barking, whining, tail whipping. She recognized his sounds. Even five years later, hearing him long-distance, the same excitement. She never forgot.

My own recorded voice has never sounded like me to me. My pitch is higher than I hear from inside, and more quavering and monotonous.

*

Some of us have singing voices, trained and untrained. Voices with volume, sweetness, clarity and range. Others, tone deaf and unable to carry a tune, improvise in the shower or in our cars. From recordings, at least, we know the opera voices of Caruso and Pavarotti, the resonance of the Irish tenor John O'Sullivan, the blues of Billie Holiday or Nina Simone, the crooning of Frank Sinatra, the folk singing of Joan Baez and Judy Collins. A gifted singer speaks for all: magnificently different, yet the same. We also blend our different voices, bass, soprano, mezzo, tenor, in choral singing, and nowhere more wonderfully than in Beethoven's Ninth Symphony, as instrumental music yields to voice and lyrics: "*Alles menschen sind bruder.*"

We recognize the individual voices of actors (regardless of roles), public figures, newscasters and weather people, voice-over narrators and other celebrities. Think of Richard Burton, Olivier, James Earl Jones. Churchill. Martin Luther King, Jr. Think of broadcasters like Edward R. Murrow or Barbara Walters. The thunder throat of Don LaFontaine, who recorded 5000 movie trailers. Sometimes their delivery impresses us more than content; or content more than delivery. Our Presidents often need voice coaches or spokespeople or both. In most cases, natural voices are amplified and modulated, if not distorted, by electronics. Of course, purely depersonalized machine voices have their uses too: "No one can come to the phone right now."

We delight in impressionists who evoke well-known speakers, somehow capturing their inflections. Likewise we applaud the ventriloquist, as she throws her voice, and with her hidden hand opening and closing her dummy's jaw, convinces us that the dummy speaks and has its own voice and personality.

Signing is voice for the speech-and-hearing-impaired, and each speaker expresses his or her emphasis through the vocabulary and rhythms of common hand signs. A song in signs looks like ballet, at least from the waist up. When a cast of deaf actors performs an entire play in signs, their audience raises its hands and shakes them for visual applause.

*

If we speak with a common voice, we agree in will, agenda, or opinion. We may even chant in unison. The people may have a voice through elected or paid representatives ("My lawyer voiced my concerns"), the press, or social media. Give me your voice, says the politician. All in favor, say aye. Speak now or forever hold your peace. "What *she* said," he said. On the individual level, in a babble of dissent, only the loudest voice gets heard. Cup your hands, grab the microphone, or bullhorn, or megaphone. Or sometimes, a picture or action speaks louder than words. The Buddhist monk, doused in gasoline, strikes his match.

*

"An authentic/fresh/original new voice," proclaim publishers of first novelists. But what is a writing voice? There is no audible sound, except for recorded books. Our librarians whisper, "Silence, please!" Children are read to at first, then learn to sound out words, to read out loud, and finally to read to themselves. Words on the page, sentences, syntax, diction, punctuation, stresses and rhythms: all somehow combine. We make sense of them.

Experienced authors tell their students to find their own voices. F. Scott Fitzgerald advised his daughter: "You learn by trying the sound and stance of other writers. You develop an ear, through your reading and imitating, for how good writing is supposed to sound." But if we absorb the manners of other writers and follow only their eyes, ears, and values, we end up doing impressions, if not deliberate parodies. Hemingway warns his acolyte Arnold Samuelson: "don't ever imitate anybody. All style is, is the awkwardness of a writer in stating a fact. If you have a way of your own, you are fortunate, but if you try to write like somebody else, you'll have the awkwardness of the other writer as well as your own"—a lesson Hemingway may have learned from sounding too much like Sherwood Anderson in "My Old Man." As Anne Lamont puts it in her writing manual *Bird by Bird:* "The truth of your experience can only come through in your own voice."

"Voice" for some critics refers to style, Cicero's or Seneca's, ornate or plain, although A. Alvarez warns us about mistaking "mere style for voice" (*The Writer's Voice*). Still other critics equate voice with vision, or persona, or the "implied author." For Wayne C. Booth, "A work of fiction has the sense not only of timbre and tone of a speaking voice, but of a total human presence."

Along with the individual, whole populations, otherwise submerged or marginalized, can be voiced as literature. One such voice represents and encourages others, speaking for and to, and granting due regard: Zora Neale Hurston's, say. Working-class voices, women's voices, immigrant voices, a new generation's voices; the formerly unspeaking or unheard.

*

And have I found mine? Does it matter, or is it lost in the crowd or in a wilderness?

EEEEE, AAAAAA, I practice, hoping to improve. Yawn, relax the throat. Try to hold middle C. Use a kazoo-like sound and keep the sound in front of my mouth. Practice up the scale using the kazoo sound and then breathe and slide down. Exclaim, "Hey, you!" Slow down my rate of talking in order to better coordinate my breathing and phonating.

This viscera of self. This living flesh, pink and animate, glistening. Speak your mind. Look in your heart and write. These neurons. Synapses. Feelings. This wonder and this enterprise.

On Time

When Orlando meets a cross-dressed Rosalind in *As You Like It,* she demands "what is't o'clock?" and he replies, taking her for an adolescent page, "There's no clock here in the forest." This idea is echoed by Hal in *Henry IV,* Part One, when Falstaff is introduced with the yawning question, "What time of day is it, lad?" to which Hal responds: "Unless hours were cups of sack, and minutes capons, and clocks the tongues of bawds ... I see no reason why thou shouldst be so superfluous to demand the time of day." The tavern, like the forest, like the play itself, is supposed to be an escape from the world of duty and cares.

Rosalind goes on to establish her wit by commenting on time's relativity: "Time travels in divers paces with divers persons." For a young maid, for instance, "time trots hard withal" between her engagement and marriage; a week seems seven years. Time ambles with the rich, who needn't work. Time gallops with a thief to the gallows, who thinks he arrives there too soon. Later, she/he advises a proud shepherdess, "Sell when you can, you're not for all markets." Natural time is further contrasted to clock time by both fool and cynic: "We ripe and ripe, then rot and rot," muses Touchstone, inspiring Jacques's set piece on the seven ages of man: "Sans teeth, sans eyes. Sans taste, sans everything."

Falstaff's tavern time yields to that of nation. On the field of honor, when Hal needs a pistol and instead Falstaff draws and offers a bottle of sack, Hal dismisses him: "What is it a time to jest and dally now?" And the last words of Hal's rival, Hotspur, who has lived primarily for honor, are that "life, time's fool ... must have a stop."

In the tragedies, bad timing and failed communication result in catastrophe: Romeo's failure to get the Friar's message, Juliet's reviving from seeming-death a moment too late; Emilia's interruption of

Othello, too late; Cleopatra's false report of death, and then of life, too late; the reprieve of Cordelia's execution, too late.

And most disturbing of all, perhaps, in regard to clashing aspects of time, are Macbeth's attempts to force natural time, which demands reproduction for a future, into personal time. Only with Macbeth's death can Scotland rejoice: "The time is free."

*

In his memoir *Crabcakes* (1998), James Alan McPherson contrasts machine time with human time. He has invited Japanese visitors to meet him for dinner at an Iowa City restaurant, but arrives three hours late. The visitors, who have eaten without him and now are leaving, are deeply offended. He then takes years to fully explain and apologize. "Our time-sense, like yours, has of necessity been different from that of the West. Perhaps the difference resides in our African genes, or perhaps it derives from the emotional adjustments we have had to make, over the centuries, in order to survive in such a brutal contest as this one. We once evolved our own time-sense. We called it CPT, or 'Colored People's Time.' This was a time sense which once ranged uniformly through our feelings, in defiance of the illusions imposed by Eastern, Central, Mountain, Pacific, Daylight Savings, and all the other time meridians east or west of Greenwich. This private time-sense had to do with the quality of our feelings, *with the health of our souls.* It was experiential, sacred time, as opposed to tick-tock clock time: *'I promised to be there at 6:45, but another person, a brother, was bleeding, and he came to me, expecting me to open up my heart and let him in....'"*

*

Time is money, we say; we spend, we save. Time waits for no man. Carpe diem! "Had we but world enough and time / This coyness, lady, were no crime" (Marvell). Time flies. Or stands still, or seems to. Waste of time. Quality time. In our time. The time of our lives (our most enjoyable moment). Prime time. Stop-time in music. Keeping time (rhythm). The test of time. Killing time. Biding time. Buying time. Stealing time. Whiling away the hours. Making time (Tim O'Brien abandons his writing career to parent his young children; as did McPherson to be present for his daughter). For everything there is a season (Ecclesiastes). "Eterne in mutability" (Spenser). Showtime! Time to deliver. Now and forever hold your peace. Hard time (both as in prison and in making something difficult). Time heals all wounds. Make up for lost time. Beat the clock. Watch the clock. In the nick of time. All in good time. Timely. Timeless. Timeworn. High time.Leisure time (thank you, industrial revolution, for time-saving conveniences; thank you, high tech). Pastime. Time on our hands. Time out. Out of time.

*

If I email my son in Bali, New Guinea, on Sunday in Boston, it is his Monday; my winter, his summer. Space is time. Longitudes determine time zones, and latitudes the seasons. Bali is some 8,800 miles from Boston, its time zone a day ahead of Boston's, and its latitude south rather than north of the equator. If I flew, I would leave Boston at noon, Saturday, and arrive there on Monday morning. Actual time in flight, at 500 mph, some 21 hours; price one-way, $1200. Light years. Light from that galaxy, those stars, is from millions of years ago.

*

Our moon orbits the earth, which orbits the sun, while our whole galaxy drifts in the Milky Way. Seasons. Winter solstice. Days and nights. Our measures of organic and geological life. Breathing in and out: how many breaths? How many heartbeats? What pulse rate? How many cycles of sleep and waking? How many years? Birthdays, death days. Eat, digest. Repetitions. Menstrual cycles. Cycles of desire. Gestation. Things grow; children grow, their heights measured on our doorjamb. In work and career, deadlines, projects in progress, completed, forgotten. Agendas. Wear and tear. Lifespans for different species and creatures. The new flock of birds, the robin nesting outside our window. Teaching, the semesters' clock, twenty-five new

20-somethings, each fall, each spring. Names change, faces, selves; I change. Their youth is the constant.

*

We speak of life journeys, which we try to measure as passages: childhood, adolescence, youth, adulthood, parenthood, grand-parenthood; pick a number. From the traveler's perspective, time blurs past like nearby landscape, moves more slowly at a middle distance, and seems fixed on the horizon. What's past and passing and to come. There is the self and the times. In personal time, we think of our dead, our parents, siblings, loved ones and friends. We have our memories of each, as persons, supported and prompted by artifacts, by documents, by photographs and films (as time passes the faces, costumes, and settings grow stranger and stranger, more fixed and quaint); we have our family legends. We dream of those as yet unmet, unborn. But then, also, there's cultural time. Collective time. Decades. Presidents. Wars. Achievements and events that touched all of us, or do touch, or will. News time (breaking and old); historical time; Biblical time. Geological time. The backwards and abysm of time. The principles of progress and decay. The species too. Evolution. Devolution. Extinction. We call them eons and ages. Life on earth. Ordovician. Devonian. Permian. Triassic. Cretaceous. 440 million years ago, 251 million, 66 million. Man's ancestors, smart apes, 10 million year ago. Neanderthals, 500,000 years ago. Homo sapiens, 200,000 years ago. Modern humans, perhaps 50,000 years ago. Our entire existence, our longevity as a species, is barely an instant in time out of mind.

*

I can't grasp, finally, the latest theories and philosophies about time, summarized here: https://plato.stanford.edu/entries/time/. We consider time as a "measurable duration," which is the whole point of clocks (whether sundial, hour glass with sand, water clock, windup, electronic, or atomic, analog or digital). We take our pulses as beats per minute. That 80-year-old has lived for 29,200 days. But parse the notions of past, present, future, of tense itself; of progress and decline; of change, succession, and motion; of Providence, foreknowledge, fate and free will: and I'm lost. Duration (from eons, lifetimes, seasons, days and hours and minutes, to milliseconds, to attoseconds) seems as reducible as particles of matter. Experience vanishes into idea. What measure or duration divides "present" from "past"? Is the present all there is, encompassing the past and future? Is the ordering of time only a function of neurology? How do we account for change itself? For growth? Decay? For a ten-minute mile or a ten-thousand mile flight? Why, beginning in the 1980s, do writers insist on telling stories in the present tense? "I wake and am a cockroach." Is all we know phenomenal, surprising and inexplicable? How do we connect then, now, and later? Is the flow of time a trick of perception, like the blur of cinematic frames? Is the notion of self as changeable as selves, so that history becomes more imagined than true and the truest story one that admits to relativity? "If I had been younger," writes Alice Munro, "I would have figured out a story ..." [an easy, sentimental version of known facts]. "Later I might have believed" [a more cynical version, concerning failures to communicate]. "Now I no longer believe that people's secrets are defined and communicable, or their feelings full-blown and easy to recognize" ("The Stone in the Field").

*

I anticipate. I plan and prepare. I rehearse a coming event in action or in mind, and when the moment arrives, and it is all happening, I'm surprised, sometimes. Sometimes the experience is more, less, better, or worse than the imagining. And then there's my memory of it afterwards—not just the eternal instant, but the flow of that happening, those five seconds or so, that hour, that day. Not the instant of a photograph. Not the sequence of instants of a video recording. But experience in full texture, fully recalled, more like a place than a time. We marry. Our children are born. I find a livelihood and mission. I mount the bungee scaffold and leap, with my elastic tether. A chapter is finished, a book. Life's conditions alter. Rewards. Disappointments. A death. A loss. An accident or health problem. Vicissitudes.

*

Alzheimer and dementia patients lose their sense of time. They can't remember loved ones or friends. They grow confused about the date, the day of the week, the season. They need fixed routines and lose their sense of duration. If you leave them for a moment, they think you've been gone all day, or that you're never coming back.

In his final years, after publishing his collection of essays, *A Region Not Home* (2000), McPherson developed dementia. He stopped traveling, writing, and teaching, and from 2010 until his death in 2015, suffered accidents, underwent various operations, and was confined to an assisted-care facility. Though we had been collaborators and personal friends, we lost phone and written contact. Friends in Iowa City kept me informed, and finally I flew from Boston to visit him in 2013. The facility was locked, presumably to prevent residents from wandering off. David Hamilton, a retired professor and former editor of *The Iowa Review,* and I signed in, found McPherson ready, and signed him out for the day. With Hamilton as host, and driving us around, McPherson seemed himself. We had our personal connection. He was witty and joking as ever, as generous and alert about people and curious about the times. It was one of his good days. We met Allen Gee, his former student, friend, and official biographer later that afternoon for a Thai dinner. We talked about teaching Shakespeare and the word "prolepsis," and when I praised his own essay about Othello, he asked: "Did I write that?" Allen Gee chimed in, "You did. It's called 'Three Great Ones of the City.'" And me: "I use it all the time, Jim. You see Othello in terms of his Levantine lineage and ethical system, symbolized by the handkerchief, and you end up comparing him to O. J. Simpson." "I do?" he asked. "I said that?" He enjoyed hearing about himself, with bemused wonder and pride, as if the self we described were some unknown, close relation.

*

Time "dilates" in space, we've discovered (https://en.wikipedia.org/wiki/Time_dilation). The clocks in the orbiting International Space Station are slower than those on earth. Since the ISS astronauts are moving faster than we do on earth, they age more slowly. On return from a six-month tour, they will have aged only a fraction less than we have, but scientists predict dramatic differences after, say, a trip to Mars and back. It's conceivable that after still farther, faster travel, future astronauts could return physically younger than their children, or even after the lifetimes of everyone they'd left.

*

We resist aging, at least once we reach our prime. Where my seven-year-old granddaughter yearns for the status of her adolescent sister, 40-somethings celebrate the cult of youth. We fight our body clocks with cosmetics, hair dye, exercise, plastic surgery, and drugs. We also resist adult responsibilities, like Peter Pan, and seek to remain free. Live for the moment! Gather ye rosebuds! Youth's a stuff that won't endure, except in Shangri-La. Even our visions of an afterlife assume a return to our prime. But who wants a perpetual present, really? We strive to adjust seasonal extremes with heat or a/c, yes. We look to cryogenics to freeze our present bodies and wake them in some future where medicine has cures for all disease, if not for mortality itself. But imagine a world without aging. Or always high noon. Always Spring. Time passes, but without measure or change. No progress. No decay.

*

The Enlightenment Deists, such as Benjamn Franklin, John Adams, and Thomas Jefferson, saw God as the divine watchmaker, who created the universe, set it going, and then stepped aside. The clock's natural laws were never changed or suspended by the maker. Through reason, men could be morally improved (see Franklin's list of daily virtues). Social justice made sense. However, while the clock was perpetual, lives were not.

Laurence Sterne's *Tristram Shandy* (1759–67) plays with the Deistic model. Tom Clark comments (http://tomclarkblog.blogspot.com/2010/08/unwinding-clock-time-in-tristram-shandy.html): "The strategies of *extension, elaboration, complication, equivocation, prolongation, procrastination, prevarication, teasing, lengthening, stretching out*—the strategies, in short, of this most digressive of novels—can be seen to have a common logical basis in the desire to retard an ending, not only of a novel, but of its author's existence."

*

Boethius (translated by Chaucer) defended free will by contrasting divine and human perspectives. God's present was eternal, and simultaenously contained the past and future: "as from a lofty mountain-top above all." For mortals, time was local: "just as you can see things in this your temporal present, so God sees all things in His eternal present." To see is not to cause. Therefore God does not "determine" our individual choices and their outcomes. We remain responsible. "If Providence sees an event in its present, that thing must be, though it has no necessity of its own nature. And God looks in His present upon those future things which come to pass through free will." At best, I understand this through the analogy to story-telling, but only partly. Chaucer's narrator knows that Troilus will lose Criseyde, but sympathetically imagines his falling in love. "So long as the future is not known to participants in the action, they can act as if they were free," comments Morton Bloomfield ("Distance and Predestination in Troilus and Criseyde"). In the end, Troilus's spirit ascends through the spheres "and joins with his author in finding what peace can be found in a pagan heaven."

*

If wisdom accrues from lessons and examples, then both individuals and societies should become wiser over time. We should stand on the shoulders of our forebears; learn, progress and grow. Or not. Civilizations fall. Languages die. Ignoring history, we do repeat it. The glory that was Greece and grandeur that was Rome declined into the Middle Ages.

And then there's also future shock. Times too present to imagine; change too complex and sudden to process. Information overload. New powers and old weaknesses. "The future is now," boasts Honeywell. But as change accelerates, generation gaps become decade gaps or less. Those born to new circumstances adapt, but their elders feel overwhelmed. The old wisdoms don't apply. The nuclear age. Birth control. Comptuters. The internet. Manned space flight. Social revolutions. New customs. Unforeseen complications. Life-prolonging medical advances. Globalization. Artificial intellgence. Robotics. Virtual reality. We can't know the future, but try to prepare. Fossil fuels dwindle as energy needs climb. Carbon emissions affect ozone depletion and global warming. Populations increase out of proportion to food and water supplies. Still how can we agree on the wisest actions to take? How can we believe?

*

British Victorians "felt the menace of the time as much as its promise," according to Jerome Buckley in *The Triumph of Time* (1966), but by mid-twentieth century, after two World Wars, the Depression, the Holocaust and the Bomb, we moderns were living "with the idea of a present decadence … And [our] visions of the future no longer evoked the bucolic utopia … but instead the grotesque perspectives of a Brave New World."

In postmodern times (those of my generation's majority), we've suffered American reverses in Vietnam and the Midde East. Poverty, racism, sexism, imperialism, oppression, and extremism persist. Yet we've also witnessed hopeful reforms and revolutions, notably those of civil rights, feminism, and the sexual revolution. The Cold War ended. Our technological and scientific advances have taken us into space, as well as into the nature of matter itself and the mysteries of minds and bodies. Our perspectives are more molecular, multicultural and global than ever.

Before the onset of his dementia, whenever McPherson visited Boston (he had friends nearby and his daughter went to Tufts), we discussed the state of our culture and times. We collaborated in editing several issues of *Ploughshares* and an anthology, *Fathering Daughters: Reflections By Men* (1998), where we asked writer-fathers about the perpexities of parenting daughters during decades of questioning, polarization, and social change. McPherson envisioned a future with "elbow room" and the emergence of an "omni-American" identity, an identity that "operates beyond race and class and sexual orientation"; however, when we talked, he dwelt on signs of decadence, moral dandyism, and materialism on every side and asked woefully what would become of us? As if in call and response, I'd counter with my own stubborn hope for what he called transcendence. The better way.

*

I believe in moments out of time. Art. Vision. Epiphanies. Walter Pater called them "profoundly signficant and animated instants, a mere gesture, a look, a smile, perhaps—some brief and wholly concrete moment—into which, however, all the motives, all the interests and effects of a long hisotry, have condensed themselves, and which seem to absorb past and future in an intense consciousness of the present."

What about the *present?* Live for the moment, some say, as if there were no tomorrow. Live for sensation. Poetry, however, is emotion recollected in tranquility. We need time to share forever the moment's meaning, while the moment itself is fleeting. As for tranquility, many seek that in nature, the heart's forest, rather than in frenetic living. Perhaps that's the idea of resting for a seventh day. Or of practicing meditation techniques, breath in, breath out, empty the mind; ignore outside distractions and demands, focus on being fully present, the here, the now. Think of Thoreau's search for essentials and his refusal to "live what was not life." Think of Anderson's "The Untold Lie" in *Winesburg, Ohio:* "The whole world seemed to Ray Pearson to have become alive with something just as he and Hal had suddenly become alive when they stood in the corn field staring into each other's eyes." Lose yourself to find yourself.

No time like the present, we say (meaning seize the day). "Gone in the instant of becoming," says William James.

*

I loves ya, tomorrow!

Oh, I believe in yesterday!

Just in time, you found me just in time.

Forever I'll be true!

These are the good old days.

We're gonna rock around the clock tonight.

O lente, lente currite, noctis equi!

*

I retired from teaching recently, but still I need time to write about time. Thoughts rise. I ransack my reading life, revisit passages and quotes that I've savored. The field of meaning grows. I brave Wikipedia, following tangents and associations. I read more. I try to be well-informed, playful, and intuitive. Meanwhile, the season turns, nearby trees drop their leaves; I rake and rake. I bag the leaves and put them out for Friday pick-up. Day by day, the weekends come. I work out in the gym from 2 to 3 p.m. My wife keeps to her busy work schedule. A right-wing President is elected. Thanksgiving comes and passes, with our trip to my son's life now in New Jersey. I go to readings and book launches by friends. My calendar has its demands. As does my body. The moon brightens to full and wanes. A cold front arrives. There are many clocks in my forest.

*

Absorbed in writing, I look up, and hours have passed.

My five-year-old wristwatch fails and I buy a new one, pleased to wake up in the night, push the button, and see its face glow green. 3:21 a.m.!

Our numbered days. We can't know how many we have, each of us, before time swallows all, including our thoughts about time.

On Folly

Ignorance may be bliss, yet still we reach for knowledge, if not wisdom; listen to serpents and forget the Gardener's warnings. We play with fire. We experiment. This is our nature. We make dumb mistakes, like a kid putting a fork into a electric outlet. Or my sixteen-year-old Ruth driving to CT the first night she had her license, to pick up a boyfriend, while telling us she was at a sleepover nearby; then skidding in rain on an exit curve, breaking her arm and totaling our car.

We make bad choices. We make short-sighted, bad bargains. We should know better, but we're easily led by impulse or deceived by others. We see the wallet with money sticking out, but as we reach, it's jerked away on a hidden string. Who knew? We're on candid camera. We learn to forgive ourselves. We pray to be forgiven our debts as we forgive our debtors; our trespasses, as we forgive those who trespass against us.

Some synonyms for Fool emphasize low intelligence—Dope. Dunce. Blockhead. Stupe. Dupe. Sucker. Clown. Butt. Ass. Laughingstock. Idiot. Moron. Nincompoop. Retard. Dimwit (DeWitt). Bear of little brain. Bobo. Meathead. Oaf. Pawn. Buffoon. Zany. Bozo. Lout. Dipshit. Dork—while others emphasize intelligence suppressed, misled, un- or misinformed—Loser, All varieties of drunkard (Lush. Sop. Sot. Souse. Boozer. Alkie). Stoner. Rube. Dick-brain. Asshole. Jerk—; and still others the mischievousness, agility, and poise of wit—Madcap. Knave. Joker. Mocker, Prankster, Tease. Lord of Misrule.

To err, to wander or deviate from true north is human. We're *errant*. We lose our moral compass. We're erratic. We can even err on the side of caution. Of course, there is comic folly, tragic folly, and tragicomic folly, depending on outcomes. Can and do we learn from our mistakes?

Is't possible to be what he is and know what he is? Is wisdom (*wis* meaning aware, and *dom* meaning doom or judgment) futile?

The goddess Folly in Erasmus's *In Praise of Folly* protests that without her there would be no marriage or children. "Mother nature gave the human race more passion than reason.... Wisdom is no other than to be governed by reason, while folly is to be swayed by the power of the passions.... [Jupiter] relegated reason to a narrow corner of the head, and left all the rest of the body to the passions."

In turn, Shakespeare's ass-headed Bottom responds to the Queen of the Fairies's declaration of love in *A Midsummer Night's Dream:* "Methinks, mistress, you should have little reason for that. And yet, to say truth, reason and love keep little company together nowadays" (both characters, of course, are figments of the writer's imagination, which only a fool would take seriously). "Lord, what fools these *mortals* be," says the *im*mortal Puck to his Fairy Master, King Oberon—sounding wise, though Puck is sometimes both mistaken and mischievous, and Oberon, like Zeus or Jupiter, is over-proud and quarreling with his Queen over a mortal page.

I try to get my students into Shakespeare's (and Erasmus's) mood by sketching a crude blackboard version of a noted Renaissance painting titled *Three Fools.* The frame shows a donkey head (Bottom) and a jester with cap and bells (Puck). Where is the third fool?

In the final act of *Midsummer,* the newly wedded aristocrats watch a badly written love tragedy put on by clueless tradesmen. The on-stage audience of lovers ridicules the performance, as if forgetting their own recent mishaps and vulnerabilities. Puck goes on to underscore this irony in the uber-play's epilogue. *We,* Shakespeare's audience, shouldn't take offense. His actors are mere shadows, and this mirror of universal folly is "no more yielding but a dream."

Ridicule assumes immunity, hence superiority, but who is immune?

The audience may be, for now. The prankster may be as she watches her victim reach for the wallet, which she jerks away with her string. But can we laugh at ourselves? Can we take a joke? You hide behind the door and as I enter what I take for an empty room, you go Boo! startling me. For an instant, I'm ready to throttle you. I want revenge. That's not funny, I say.

There's a fine line between good-natured kidding and meanness. Richard III and Iago are jokers too, superior, they think, in wit and wisdom. Wise-guys. "Was ever woman in this humor won?" Richard believes that "dissembling nature" has made a fool of him, with his hunched back, and he sets out to make fools of family, friends, and society as a whole (including the audience), only to prove to be his own worst fool.

As opposed to such wise-guys, the wise fool serves to wise up others, usually authority figures such as kings, generals, or patriarchal fathers, who have sway over their subjects, wives, children, and their social inferiors. The wise fool shares this role with entertainers, artists, poets, playwrights, players, and story-tellers. In Latin, French, and Spanish, *narra* means to fool, a meaning carried in our word *narrator.*

"At court, every famous king had his own fool," writes Barry Sanders in his study of laughter, *Sudden Glory,* "a licensed madman who gave the king both advice and entertainment, provided his remarks did not get too personal." An historical example is Will Sommers in the court of Henry VIII. In Shakespeare's comedies, Puck, Touchstone, and Feste are outright jesters, while Falstaff and Lucio are corrupt gentlemen who play the role, and Autolycus an ousted jester who survives as a petty thief and con-man. Each wise fool is also contrasted to a witless clown or rube figure (Bottom, William, Andrew, Poins, Bernadine, and the Shepherd's son). Similar pairings are found in such modern acts as Abbott and Costello, Laurel and Hardy, Martin and Lewis, Cheech and Chong, and explored in circus clowning in Fellini's 1970 film *The Clowns.* Somewhat like a therapist who has been required to undergo therapy before being licensed, the wise fool is aware of her/his own folly, while commenting on and treating that of others. I don't know if Freud saw himself in this way; probably not, although he had his theories about laughter, jokes, and identity.

In my personal life, I'm often a fool. Sometimes I exaggerate some habit on purpose, or try to be silly to make my wife and kids laugh. Other times, like wise fools, I suppose, they mock my unintentional folly.

My wife, for instance, tells our kids a story from our living together before we were married. She came home late from work and found that I'd made creamed hamburger, leaving half in the pan for her. She tasted it, thought it looked grainy, then saw the jar of plaster of Paris on the counter. Yes, I'd used that. It was flour. I'd found it on the overhead shelf and added milk and seasoning, as always. We called the ER, and were told after some consultation and laughter in the background, that I should eat all the liquid Jello we could mix, which would keep the plaster inside from setting. Moral: even though I'd survived as a bachelor, I'd proved an incompetent cook.

Or another, which I'll tell on myself, from before I met Connie. In the late 1960s, the new fashion of going braless prompted me to wonder about a distant young woman walking in my direction: was she braless or not? As we grew closer, like sexual gunslingers, I could see she was. I admired the soft bounce of her breasts and the suggestion of nipples. But then her eyes met mine. "DeWitt?" she asked. It was Shawna, after a makeover and wearing shades. Shawna with whom I had broken up a few weeks before, put out of mind, and hadn't seen since. Shawna whom I had met at a cruising buddy's party and dated; Shawna, whom I had dumped because I didn't really like her body or her mind, but had tried to let down gently by saying that we were getting serious and I wasn't ready to be serious, so it was better if we stopped seeing each other. The different outfit, hairstyle and dark glasses had fooled me. Chagrined, "Hope you're good," I stammered.

"Oh, I am," she said, and kept on going. Moral: I was a lust-driven, objectifying jerk.

I can be as pompous as Polonius. My daughter invited the same boy from Connecticut to visit and stay overnight on our downstairs couch. Connie and I slept upstairs, as did Ruth, but when I woke to distant laughter, I realized that Ruth had sneaked back down. I headed down myself, barefoot, stairs creaking, and confronted them. "With freedom comes responsibility," I intoned. "I just want you to hear that." Then I turned, indignant, and stomped back upstairs. Ten minutes later, my daughter followed.

I tried to teach my son frugality. He was thirteen. His printer was out of ink and he wanted a new cartridge, which cost a third of what the printer itself had cost—a marketing gimmick I had seen coming, and the reason that I'd kept a refill kit; but having closed myself in the bathroom, when I tried refilling his cartridge, the kit's hypodermic was blocked and backfired in my face; black ink everywhere. My son, his girlfriend and Connie looked in and laughed. "Design flaw," I explained; and after cleaning up, I went to buy new cartridges. My son to this day unwittingly endorses my father's maxim that penny wise is pound foolish.

Later, I was mocked at home for buying a hundred dollar snow rake—an aluminum contraption with a T-shaped solid blade at the top and five-foot long sections that snap together until it can reach the peak of our roof. We had no apparent need for it, but then several winters later we got buried by record accumulations; ice dams and roof collapses were in the news. I assembled my rake, the only one in our neighborhood, and holding it at my waist like a deep-sea fishing rod, I pulled down avalanches from both sides of my roof. Even my neighbor asked to borrow it. A fool redeemed!

My executive father's biggest folly was his alcoholism before I was born—both a condition and choice, I thought, like his flaccid, overweight body (210–260 lbs, depending on dieting) and his emphysema. A chain smoker of 3 to 4 packs per day, he fell into coughing fits with each light-up. He'd been to AA, my mother told me, undergone therapy, and afterwards settled into being the awkward, withdrawn father I knew: complacent, habit-driven, vain, close-minded, prejudiced, and preoccupied with money, class and status. He sneaked cake between meals (we'd hear the tell-tale ring of the cake cover). He refused to say "Please pass the salt," instead of "Is that the salt over there?" He dreamed of owning a Cadillac, but could only afford Buicks. We kept the story of his illness from friends and relatives. When he himself told me about it, he said that alcohol had damaged his brain and that my mother was remarkable for sticking with him through it all. He'd always be grateful. He enjoyed taking us for Sunday drives around our suburb and "snooping"—peering in at other supposedly successful lives—almost as much he enjoyed the privacy of our own yard.

As I mocked my father, so my loved ones mock me.

Errors, a forgiveable common denominator ("Anyone could have made the same mistake," we allow), elide into the offensive, the criminal and pathological (not so forgiveable, at least without some treatment or reformation, as in my father's case), and from there into sin (welcome to the Inferno, with its hierarchy from venal to mortal); comic errors, into tragic. Romeo sees himself as Fortune's Fool, but fails to recognize Juliet's reviving. Emilia blames Othello for murdering Desdemona: "O, gull. O dolt, / As ignorant as dirt!" And Othello realizes that he has loved "not wisely but too well!" Lear mistakes the true love of Cordelia for ingratitude, while embracing the flattery of her harpy sisters. It takes the therapeutic zingers of his "all-licensed fool" to awaken regret: "Dost thou call me fool, boy? … I did her wrong." Lear's agon progresses through rage, injustice, sympathy, madness, and forgiveness to a fuller recognition both of error and of love. Even Macbeth finally realizes that he's been fooled by the witches' double meanings and the promises of recorded history, which is itself a tale told by an idiot. His ideas of grace and glory have proved as foolish as Malvolio's dream of becoming a Count.

I could've had a V8!

My greatest folly may be my love of literature. The dream of writing well. My turning from family and friends to sit at this solitary desk. My dream of being capable of words that strangers won't willingly let die.

If the fool would persist in folly he would become wise, says Willliam Blake.

On Appetite

For food. For fame. For art. For company. For power. For knowledge. For love. For glory. For adventure. For entertainment. For revenge. For money. For life. From the Latin *appetare:* to seek for, and *appetitus:* to desire for.

Your eyes are bigger than your stomach. Biting off more than you chew. Clean your plate. I binge on wafer-thin Pringles, unable to eat just one. It's better to eat smaller portions more often than to stuff yourself. Our oldest brother, Jack, however, the only naturally thin one in our family, came home for Thanksgiving from his life 2000 miles away. He did the carving. We marveled while he out-ate all of us, three or four portions of turkey, gravy, stuffing, cranberry sauce, and even the roasted vegetables. Then, stomach distended, he lay down on the living-room sofa and fell asleep.

Samuel Johnson found the "hunger of the imagination" to be our torment and blessing. We seek to fill up the "vacuity of life," and fail. "Few of the hours in life are adequate to the mind of man.... recollection and anticipation fill up almost all our moments" (*The Achievement of Samuel Johnson* by Walter Jackson Bate, p. 64).

Forbidden fruit: Eve's temptation in Eden; and later a gift for teachers. Cleopatra, that dish for the gods, makes "hungry where most she satisfies." Falstaff, both glutton and epicure, is glorified by such insults as "sweet beef" and "a manning tree ox with a pudding in his belly."

Feast your eyes.

The infant's howl. 11% of the world is starving (http://www. worldhunger.org/2015-world-hunger-and-poverty-facts-and-statistics/); meanwhile others, overweight and tempted by abundance, take diet pills to curb their appetites.

Some of us are picky eaters. I have my favorites (turkey, ham, beef, lamb, corn, carrots, tomatoes, potatoes, eggs, cheese, spinach, peas), tolerances (sweet potatoes, eggplants, squash), and aversions (fish, asparagus, cabbage, squash, kale, liver, lima beans). Some tastes are cultural, if not dietary, as in Spielberg's *Indiana Jones and The Temple of Doom* film where Kate Capshaw and the audience are dis-*gusted* by cooked snakes and beetles (https://www.youtube.com/watch?v=3MgyRO3c870)—a challenge beyond even Anthony Bourdain's relativism.

Appetites collide in Fielding's *Tom Jones*, Book 9, Ch. 5, as the hero feasts with Mrs. Waters at an inn: "how much soever we may be in love with an excellent sirloin of beef, or bottle of Burgundy … yet do we not smile nor ogle, nor dress, nor flatter … to gain the attention of the said beef…. The contrary happens in that love which operates between persons of the same species…." In Tony Richardson's film, Joyce Redman suggestively mimics Albert Finney's tearing and gnawing his meat, which escalates into a duet of sucking oysters and burying faces in fruit; and ends in their tumbling into bed (http://entertainment.time.com/2012/01/06/top-10-memorable-movie-eating-scenes/slide/tom jones/). "The heart of Mr. Jones was entirely taken," wrote Fielding, "and the fair conqueror enjoyed the usual fruits of her victory."

Haute cuisine. The aesthetics of food. My son, who for years favored McDonalds, after reading Eric Schlosser's *Fast Food Nation,* began to follow cooking shows, from *The Galloping Gourmet* and *Julia Child* to *The Iron Chef.* Food as art comes in small portions, as enticing to the eye as complex and subtle in flavor. Gourmands savor more than they crave. Appetites can be gross or refined.

We may be hungry, but appetite, like desire, is subject to imagination; and appetizers serve as a kind of foreplay. "Yum, that was appetizing…. That was awful, bland. Not appetizing at all." Appearances matter. Seasoning, smells ("That smells delicious!"), herbs and sauces enhance the tasteless or otherwise unappealing. Mouths water. We're stimulated.

As a teen, my sister refused to drink milk I'd turned green with food coloring; but blindfolded, she couldn't taste any difference.

As an adult, she suffered from thyroid medication that eliminated taste, and her favorite food became celery because of the crunch.

The epitome of non-appetizing is a formula of glucose, salts, amino aides, lipids and added vitamins and minerals delivered by IV.

*

Diets can be weight-gaining or -losing, high or low protein, meat-eating or vegetarian, processed or prepared, liquid or solid, balanced or steady, healthy or not. "I am a great eater of beef," says Sir Andrew, "and I believe that does harm to my wit." Our diet of junk foods, designed and consumed for pleasure, is high in sugars, fat and salt. When did nervous eating evolve? Popcorn at the movies; chips and snacks as we watch suspenseful sports or thrillers on TV? The munchies. The craves. Eating for anxiety, entertainment, or out of boredom, rather than for sustenance.

Appetites can be insatiable or sated. But gluttony can't be confused with destitution. "I'm so hungry I could eat a horse!" The poor eat dog food and stone soup. Dumpster divers compete with rats. Think of Knut Hamsun's writer in Hunger: chewing on wood chips, sucking a pebble, biting his finger; so starved that when he does eat, he can't help vomiting; and all of this self-inflicted, of course, pride-inflicted, as he insists only on writing for livelihood. Says Paul Auster; "it's almost a moral, intellectual and aesthetic experiment he's playing out within his own body" (*The Art of Hunger*, 1993). Yet he's no hunger artist ("Just try to explain to anyone the art of fasting!" writes Kafka), anorexic, or hunger-striker for a cause, like Gandhi.

*

Most of us consider cannibalism unnatural. One exception is Montaigne: "I am sorry that, seeing so clearly into their faults, we should be so blind to our own" ("Of Cannibals"). Unnatural and monstrous also describes murder, incest, rape, sadomasochism, and all sorts of addictions. "Our natures do pursue, / Like rats that ravin down their proper bane, / A thirsty evil, and when we drink we die," laments Claudio in *Measure for Measure*. In *Lear*, on learning of Gloucester's blinding, Albany exclaims: "Humanity must perforce prey on itself, / Like monsters of the deep."

You look good enough to eat! I could eat you up!

The opposite of appetite is nausea. Indigestion. We can't stomach certain foods, behaviors and circumstances; our gorge rises. As does that of Jean Paul Sartre's metaphysical discontent in the post-Holocaust world of *Nausea:* "There is a white hole in the wall, a mirror. It is a trap.... The grey thing appears in it ... the reflection of my face.... It is alive. I can't say it isn't.... I see the insipid flesh blossoming and palpitating with abandon.... I draw my face closer until it touches the mirror. The eyes, nose, and mouth disappear: nothing human is left.... I have no taste for work anymore.... I have it, the filth, the Nausea."

The ancient Romans induced vomiting, finger in throat, to make room for more feasting.

Eating disorders are treated as mental illnesses: binge eating disorder, anorexia nervosa, bulimia nervosa, pica (eating dirt), rumination disorder, avoidant/restrictive food intake disorder, muscle dysmorphia (https://en.wikipedia.org/wiki/Eating_disorder). Common psychological causes include poor body- and self-image, objectification, child abuse, sexual violence, and power envy. Mary Pipher in *Reviving Ophelia* examines how "America today limits girls' development, truncates their wholeness, and leaves many of them traumatized"; and Naomi Wolf in *The Beauty Myth* attacks the obsession with female thinness: "The ideology of semi-starvation undoes feminism.... To maintain hunger where food is available, as Western women are doing, is to submit to a life state as unnatural as anything with which the species has come up yet."

*

When I'm sick, I lose mine. The sight even of my favorite foods offends me. I try not to throw up, and then I do. And afterwards, weakly, I try to start eating again, beginning with liquids, then solids, milk-toast; food that will stay down.

My older brother, Chuck, lost his appetite at age 64. Divorced, a cancer surgeon, he'd suddenly lost weight; then went out with doctor friends for dinner, ordered a steak but hardly touched it. The friends insisted he go in for a check-up; x-rays showed "more cancer than lung," and they immediately hospitalized him. He was dead five weeks later.

*

It's good for you. Just eat. Why won't you eat? Stop playing with your food. Just try it; it won't hurt to try. If you don't like it, okay, but try it first.

"He likes it! Hey, Mikey!" (Life cereal commercial, 1970s: https://youtu.be/CLQ0LZSnJFEY)

Savor. Relish. It takes life to love life.

Dig in. Have a taste.

Bon appetit!

On Grades

On the upgrade, my car labors, but not as much as the behemoth trucks I keep passing; my speed decreases, despite my pressing the gas, from 60 to 55 to 50; then I crest the hill, as do the trucks behind me finally, and on the downgrade my speed climbs to 70, and there are warning signs about braking, skidding and turnoffs. I use my motor for a brake, and the trucks go juggernauting past.

The weight and power of our vehicles determines the grade, usually the maximum is 30%. We seek the level. If a road needs to cross a mountain, we design curves and cutbacks around its steepness, back and forth. If we must, we blast rock at the top to lower a passageway, or we excavate tunnels through its mass.

*

Making the grade, we say. Upgrade (from coach to first-class, for instance, improving conditions and privileges). Degrade (to reduce, to humiliate, to lessen in strength or power). Low-grade fever. High-grade ore, or octane; Grade-A eggs, milk, or beef.

*

In schools, there are grades K through 12, meaning levels of aptitude and difficulty. Then in each grade, students are graded, measuring levels of achievement. Sometimes they are graded "on a curve," comparing their individual scores against the average for the entire class, rather than a strict standard. As they apply to college and graduate schools, they take standardized tests, which are graded, the SATs and GREs. In higher ed., where I teach, they earn grades course by course, satisfying core and major requirements, and their cumulative grade average determines scholarships, awards, graduation status (laude, cum laude, summa cum laude), and their promise for employers.

*

Graders themselves are graded (as are entire schools): from soft, easy, generous, lenient, lax, permissive, indulgent to strict, harsh, tough, demanding, hard, rigorous, challenging, No accident that fields of learning are called disciplines. In boot camp, the saying goes, a Good Joe officer can get you killed. This hurts me more than it hurts you, my mother used to say, before spanking me.

*

Teaching literature to undergraduates, I hated grading. The myth of the arbitrary—the teacher's tossing quizzes on a flight of stairs for grades—is something students mostly joke about, but for measurable learning to mean anything, students have to respect their grader. They should agree that their skills and efforts are worthwhile and fairly judged. Test questions should further insight and understanding. With essays, the grader has read their words carefully, and has identified legitimate strengths, weaknesses, and ways to improve.

I fought the chore. Procrastinated. Skimmed though their essays uncritically; then forced myself to reread and bear down with corrections and comments. Did their sentences make sense? Were they grappling with complicated questions? Did they support their assertions with key quotations and critical references? Did they think for themselves?

After five or ten papers, I'd be in my zone, but still it took me 20–30 minutes each paper. Sometimes longer. And I kept to my standard of returning them by the following class. My best students were invigorating to think with. My worst suffered writing problems so severe that I refused to grade their papers until they worked on revisions at our Learning Assistance Center.

Repeatedly our administration accused the faculty of "grade inflation," and threatened to impose quotas. Nearly half of the 1500 students each year graduate with honors.

I was part of the problem, I admit. I meant to be an easy grader because the material was hard and my courses rigorous. We covered six Shakespeare plays per semester with a graded exchange for each play; the in-class quizzes and short papers were designed to build the skills and perspectives for a fifteen-page research paper. Most of my students earned As or A-s and the rest B+s, with an occasional B. I agonized and sometimes lost sleep over whether an A- should have been a B+, or vice versa. But I did believe my grades to be fair; and even when I tried to be more strict, by my best judgment I couldn't be. My students simply were engaged, working hard, and learning well.

In graduate workshops, instead of letter grades, I wrote lengthy, detailed comments for individual stories or chapters. Unalloyed praise and the suggestion to send out for publication suggested an A. Praise mixed with suggestions for revision, an A-. Sympathetic encouragement and love for certain features, a B+. Identification of flaws in story logic, development, style, or concept, and suggestions for more study and practice of fundamentals of craft, a B or B-. Final grades could only be letters, of course. For twelve students, I gave mostly A-s. Again, I agonized.

When colleagues proposed a system of pass/fail, the students themselves insisted on grades. Funded by tuitions, our program couldn't afford to be as selective as some others, and our most talented and productive students needed to be identified, especially as they applied to PhD programs or sought teaching jobs in a market flooded by MFAs.

*

Cheating, of course, subverts any system of grading. Consider how the novelist, memoirist, and Professor Tobias Wolff portrays his younger self in *This Boy's Life*. The estranged son of a con-man, young Toby has been a delinquent screw-up in high school, but hopes to get a scholarship to the prestigious Hill School and eventually to join the ruling class. A friend who works in the high-school office smuggles him school stationery and transcript forms. "I felt full of things that had to be said, full of stifled truth.... I believed in that in some sense not factually verifiable I was a straight-A student." He forges stellar recommendations. "I wrote without heat or hyperbole, in the words my teachers would have used if they had known me as I knew myself." He scores well on a prep-school version of the SAT, is interviewed, and accepted (only to flunk out later, join the Army and serve in Vietnam; although still later, he graduates from Oxford and legitimately earns "money, a certain array of merchandise ... and the world's esteem").

In my own student career, I never was tempted to cheat or plagiarize. However, in college I was embarrassed by a professor's seriously requiring us to self-grade. I didn't know if I deserved the A I hoped for, so I put in B+, hoping that the professor would boost it higher. He didn't.

*

Falstaff flouts his society. Honor is a mere scutcheon. Discretion is the better part of valor, he asserts, playing dead as Hal defeats the rebel Hotspur; then once Hal exits, jumping up and wounding Hotspur's corpse, so that on Hal's return, he can claim that Hotspur had revived as well, that he Falstaff had finished him, and that he therefore deserves honor and reward. Hal lets him off in good humor, yet again; but when Hal becomes King later, he will flatly reject Falstaff with the equivalent of an F. Where we do we stand, I ask my students and myself; with Falstaff's vitalism, or with Hal's duty as King?

*

From 1959 to 1962, Amherst College had an Underachiever Policy. If you had proven aptitude, but you were missing classes, flunking courses, and getting into scrapes, then clearly you were squandering opportunities, or worse. You were Falstaff! *Time* magazine called it "a program to unload loafers." My freshman roommate got a mandatory one-year leave as a result (he later returned, graduated a class behind me, and became a successful gynecologist). I worried I might be another, since instead of my high school As, I nearly failed freshman

Physics and Math. But I managed to compensate in my left brain major and finally graduated Magna (meanwhile the Policy had been dropped). Still, I was chastened by other classmates clearly abler than I was, particularly George Peterson, who graduated Summa. Everything seemed easy for him, no matter what the subject, even English.

*

While Amherst's President belabored underachievers, he also joined the Presidents of Smith, U. Mass. Amherst and Mt. Holyoke College in examining "the assumptions and practices in liberal arts education"; which led to their joint founding of Hampshire College, an experiment in "alternative education." Opened in 1970, Hampshire would have no grades. No prescribed curriculum. No "silencing" of students. No culture of competition, reward or punishment. Instead of grades, students received extensive written feedback. Instead of distribution requirements, they would "build a concentration out of their interests and curiosity in consultation with advisors." They would be active "producers and creators" more than passive "consumers of information." Learning would be multi-disciplinary, "inquiry-based, discussion rich, and challenging." The capstone of learning would be the student portfolio. Over time, "graduate schools and employers [would come to] appreciate Hampshire's comprehensive narrative transcript, which [would offer] a level of detail not reflected in traditional transcripts."

Now forty-five years later, Hampshire is well-established, and known for its creative alums, particularly in film. Other colleges offering alternatives to letter grades include Brown University, where all classes can be taken as pass/fail or students can choose a system of A, B, and C grades (no minuses, no Fs recorded). Rather than relying on a transcript, Brown's students are encouraged to customize a portfolio of work that is supplemented by grades. Sarah Lawrence has both letter grades and written evaluations in a seminar-based system. In addition to narrative evaluations and capstone portfolios, Arveno

College and Fairhaven College use self-assessment as well.

*

What is our value? What is our deserving? What is our objective for ourselves and for others? Who does the evaluating and with what criteria and knowledge? What are our certified skills and credentials? Who evaluates a life or a career or both? About parenting, when I told my dying mother that she had earned an A+ in all respects, she said she only deserved an E for effort.

*

Whatever our earthly grades, we dream of heavenly ones as more profoundly just. Souls deserving of St. Peter's F's, like Dr. Faustus's, are hell-bound, while the A's get wings. Frank Capra's Clarence in *It's a Wonderful Life,* wins his promotion from second-class salvation (presumably a wingless C) to angel first-class (A).

On Courage

"Take heart," we say. Or, "she's got heart" (meaning "soul," as something more than "sympathy" or "sentiment"). "She really puts her heart into it—her work, her friendships, family life, and causes."

In Chaucer's time, "courage" and "heart" were synonyms. "So priketh hem Nature, in hir corages," he writes of his "smale foweles" in April, a meaning echoed in our word "core" (tested to her core, core self, core values). *Cor* is Latin for heart, as is *coeur* in French. Coeur de Lion.

"For he was great of heart," Shakespeare's Cassio exclaims after Othello's self-execution, an estimate rejected by feminists who view Othello only as a fool, a murderer, and even a villain.

Coaches and teachers "encourage" their athletes, dancers, writers, and students. Likewise courtships are encouraged or discouraged by one party or another. Othello was encouraged by Desdemona—"She'd come again, and with a greedy ear / Devour up my discourse."

Critics discourage and dishearten. Patrons encourage, though usually too late, as Samuel Johnson has written: "Is not a patron, my lord, one who looks with unconcern on a man struggling for life in the water, and, when he has reached ground, encumbers him with help?"

Courage also means bravery. Brave heart, we say. Or home of the brave. Native American warriors were called braves. Another synonym is "fortitude," derived from the Latin "fortis," meaning srength and endurance. A stronghold is a fort. He was well fortified with courage (or alcohol).

Nerve, we say. She's got nerve. Or, well, balls (G.I. Jane: "I got the balls"). Of course, in male mythology, "castrating bitches" overpower and tame their men, especially in 1950s fictions. "She wore the pants in the family." In Shakespeare, we've got Lady Macbeth (or seem to); while his comic shrews teach more than they dominate.

The nerve of him. That player in the '60s singles' bar (where I was shy). He saunters up to a babe talking with her girlfriend, reaches out and fingers her brooch, just over one breast. "Nice," he says. And suddenly they're talking. Fools rush in where angels fear to tread.

The red badge of courage: war, competitive sports, and maybe hunting are its usual contexts. "Heartbreak Hill," mile 22 of the Boston Marathon. The two-time women's champion, Uta Pippig, with menstrual blood streaking her legs, falls behind and struggles to keep pace, but manages 4.6 miles later to finish a close second. However, athletic endurance can't rival my wife in childbirth, I think. My older brother, a doctor, dismisses that comparison. Women don't have a choice, he says; their bodies take over. Still, I insist, the ordeal of birth is for the sake of new life, not merely for winning or setting a record. It's ironic to me that men call each other girly or sissy for being cowardly, while at the same time envying the life-creating powers of the female body (Freud calls this pregnancy envy, manifest in Dr. Frankenstein and modern cloning). And even beyond birth, true valor is shown in parenting, I believe, in nourishing—alma Mater!—in loving no matter what, and in sacrificing for the sake of others.

Courage takes belief. We face danger and pain for more than bravado or showing off. Unless we're drunk or stoned and feel invincible, in which case we don't think (intoxicate means "to poison," remember, as in "name your poison"; hence we need to be detoxed). Think of AA's serenity prayer: "God grant me the serenity to accept the things I cannot change, courage to change the things I can, and the wisdom to know the difference." The ancient Greeks grouped Fortitude, Justice, Prudence, and Temperance as the Cardinal Virtues.

Is suicide an act of bravery, as the Stoics argued (and as protesting monks and suicide bombers believe); or is it cowardice, an escape from pain (the fardels, slings and arrows that Hamlet fears)? One size can't fit all, but surely a desperate act can't be brave, since it fails belief; except perhaps for the nihilist who believes everything pointless.

The Greeks further divided courage into kinds: moral, political, and physical, although the categories mix and conflict, as in Milton's calling Cromwell "a brave, bad man." Milton also insisted that moral and political courage be shown in action, rather than inaction; nevertheless elsewhere allows that "they also serve who only stand and wait." Martin Luther King and Gandhi combined all three courages in their acts of conscience and conscientious objection. JFK praises politicians in *Profiles in Courage* (1955): "Senators of courage—men whose abiding loyalty to their nation triumphed over all other personal and political considerations, men [and women] who showed the real meaning of courage and a real faith in democracy." Political cowards, by contrast, are "a mere collection of robots dutifully recording the views of their consituents, or a gathering of time-servers skilled only in predicting and following the tides of public sentiment." And even the best trained athlete needs desire and luck to win. And not only to win: witness the Hoits finishing the Boston Marathon year after year, the father pushing his parapelegic son in a racing chair and drawing his strength from love and his son's own courage.

In *The Things They Carried,* Tim O'Brien's character, Tim O'Brien, confesses that he was about to flee to Canada to evade being drafted into the Vietnam War: "My conscience told me to run ... [but] I would go to war—I would kill and maybe die—because I was embarrassed not to ... I was a coward. I went to the war."

Hemingway prizes grace under pressure, especially in matadors, but also in writers and in how close they work to moral, spiritual, and psychological danger. The bravery of this writing, we often exclaim;

the heart! Or if not, the bravado of it, the posturing. Or no matter how graceful, we feel it is too safe. The critic Kenneth Burke echoes similar ideas with a twist, comparing the poet to "Perseus who could not face the serpent-headed monster without being turned to stone, but was immune to this danger if he observed it by reflection in a mirror. The poet's style, his form (a social idiom), is this mirror, enabling him to confront this risk, but by the protection of an indirect reflection." But is this protection more cowardly than courageous? The better part of valor is discretion?

Lorrie Moore is our laureate of phobophobia. Her typical character "didn't like to do things where the trick is not to die" and dwells on threats of cancer, aging, divorce, environmental polution, rapists, nuclear proliferation, Big Brother, and general doom. The author's coping mechanism, and often that of her characters, is that of "laugh now, think later humor," at least until the life of a baby is at risk (see her masterpiece, "People Like That Are The Only People Here: Canonical Babbling in Peed Onc"): "'Really,' the Oncologist is saying, 'of all the cancers he could get, this is probably the best.' 'We win,' says the Mother." Irony falters, however, much as it does for O'Brien's soldiers: "They used a hard vocabulary to contain the terrible softness. *Greased*, they'd say. *Offed, lit up, zapped while zipping.* It wasn't cruelty, just stage presence. They were actors."

We brave the elements and our physical limits. The blank page. The election. Aging and mortality.

Keep the faith, we tell each other. Show some backbone. Tenacity. Pluck. Boldness. Guts. True grit.

"Bravo!" we cry (Italian for brave) as we applaud performances of life and art.

O Brave We! exclaims Samuel Johnson about humanity.

Trust inspiration, wherever it leads. Be open, be vulnerable. Doubt, question, disagree. Suffer consequences.

It takes life to love life.

Both lion and chicken manage to survive.

On Bonds

As a boy, I filled a savings book with slots for quarters from my allowance, then took it to the bank and bought a $25 U.S. Savings Bond for $17.50. Ten years later, I cashed in my bond for face value, and supposedly this helped to finance World War II. If we'd lost, the bond would have been worthless: a junk bond, like Confederate currency.

A bond is a legal promise, or contract, in the financial sense. The investor buys a debt security, to be repaid after a certain term with interest. But in other senses, a bond can be spiritual. We share a bond of friendship or of blood. We enter into the bond of holy matrimony. Our word is our bond. We're bound by duty or by honor, say. Obligated. Bonds imply trust. In the Bible (Gen. 9), God makes a covenant with Noah and his descendants, symbolized by the rainbow. Humankind will never again be destroyed by water, though the fire next time remains an option.

Arrested, we call a bondsman to put up bail. We promise to show up in court. If we break our bond and skip court, the bondsman forfeits his money and puts a bounty on our heads, hoping to return us to jail and to get some money back.

Another kind of bondsman is a slave. Free men are conquered, and bound, their lives spared as long they build pyramids, row galleys, pick cotton, etc. They become beasts of burden, fed, clothed, sold, traded, and bred for profit by their masters. Bondage involves chains or ropes. We are bound, and held by force, and even if the chains or ropes are removed, still for a time there may be no freedom. Free me from my bonds! Let my people go! Bondage, however, is desired in the arena of kinky sex, where bondage (in padded handcuffs, say) mocks slavery. I'm the victim. I consent to have no consent. There's liberty in helplessness.

A vagabond is free and wayward, without a bond, allegiances or property. A husband, on the other hand, is tied to his house, his family. He is house (hus)-bound (band).

Bonded also can mean certified, as it does with whiskey that has been "aged and bottled according to a set of legal regulations … as laid out in the Bottled-in-Bond Act of 1897." Where whiskey sold as "straight" often had been watered down, flavored and colored with iodine or tobacco, or otherwise adulterated, bonding guaranteed that the liquor is "the product of one distillation season (January–June or July–December) and one distiller at one distillery. It must have been aged in a federally bonded warehouse under U.S. government supervision for at least four years and bottled at 100 (U.S.) proof (50% alcohol by volume). The bottled product's label must identify the distillery where it was distilled and, if different, where it was bottled. Only spirits produced in the United States may be designated as bonded" (Wikipedia). Thus standards are set and fraud exposed. In a similar way bond paper, made mostly from rag pulp, is watermarked.

We share bonds of commonality by species, nation, race, religion, family, and interests. As individuals, we bond together, and become allies or friends. The metaphor of attachment extends to glue. We cement one piece to another, so the two become one. We put on a clamp and give the glue time to bond under pressure; otherwise the pieces divide. Band-Aids help wounds to bond and heal; as do bandages.

Shakespeare, supposedly a shrewd investor, a sometime money-lender, son of a recusant Catholic, and himself a wayward family man, wove the thread of our subject through many of his plays. In *The Merchant of Venice*, as Marjorie Garber notes: "The concept of the bond, which both enslaves and frees, is another common feature between this play and others …" (such as *The Comedy of Errors*). Besides the stratagem of Shylock's "merry" bond, which, given luck, will put his enemy Antonio at his mercy, there are legal bonds between servingman and master; dead father, heiress and suitors; and through its charter, Venice and all its residents, regardless of creed, tribe, or culture. There are moral bonds between parent and child, husband and wife, rich friend and poor friend ("To you, Antonio,/I owe the the most, in money and in love"). Bonds of faith, Christian and Jewish; and bonds of humanity ("If you prick us, do we not bleed?"); as well as bonds of romantic love. All are tested. Not only are these bonds threatened by hypocrisy, avarice and betrayal, but even the moral bonds themselves conflict and compete. Bassanio has promised Portia never to take off his ring, but here he owes the law clerk a debt of gratitude for saving Antonio's life and the clerk (Portia in disguise) will only take the ring. As Bassanio surrenders it, he hopes that his Portia will understand. Portia's stratagem is genuinely merry, however, as she later accuses Bassanio of infidelity and pretends to her own infidelity as revenge. We're meant to enforce our claims with mercy (even if the play and Portia offend us with Shylock's forced conversion).

There's nothing merry in *Lear*, where all bonds are cracked, and also perhaps redeemed, at least in intention. In madness, Lear himself calls for doomsday, that things might change, or cease. And Gloucester echoes Thomas Hooker on the breaking of the Great Chain of Being: "Love cools, friendship falls off, brothers divide. In cities, mutinies, in countries, discord, in palaces, treason, and the bond cracked 'twixt son and father." Today we fear for the environment as well.

And what of the bond between writer and reader? "No tears in the writer, no tears in the reader," advises Robert Frost. We may expect different writers to delight and instruct; to provide escape or solace; to challenge and make us think; some, even, to "catch the conscience of the King." Aristotle had his requirements for tragedy ("an imitation of an action of high importance ... by means of pity and fear effecting its purgation of the emotions.... decent people should not be shown passing from good fortune to misfortune.... nor again should an utterly evil man fall from good fortune into misfortune"); and Shakespeare had his ("The tragic hero in Shakespeare ... need not be 'good,'" observes A. C. Bradley; "But ... he should have so much of greatness that in his error and fall we may be vividly conscious of the possibilities of human nature"); as did Arthur Miller ("the common man is as apt a subject for tragedy in its highest sense as kings were"). And what happens when the writer betrays the bond by breaking an implied promise? C. S. Lewis complains that Chaucer, in the end of *Troilus,* "spares us no detail of the prolonged and sickening process to despair.... The thing is so painful that perhaps no one without reluctance reads it twice.... We turn, for relief, to the titanic passions and heroic deaths of tragedy, because they are sublime and remote, and hence endurable. But this, we feel, goes almost beyond the bounds of art; this is treason." Other ideas about the bounds and decorums of literature have been debated in our time by Johns Gardner and Barth, among others; by canon revisionists, by the Vatican, Marxists, feminists, non-Westerners, and Minority writers such as Toni Morrison ("My project is ... to avert the critical gaze from the racial object to the racial subject"). Different situations and interests demand different bonds. Meanwhile prize committees bond contemporary writing much as we do whiskey: the Pulitzer, the National Book Award, the Booker, Oprah's Book Club, the Great Reads.

Finally, certain bonds remain sacred. Our soul is at stake, if not in a religious sense, then in our sense of self and being. My own are to my wife, family, talent, teaching, literature, fellow writers, and friends. And, I should add, to my body, since when I take it for granted, it quickly reminds me that it's not. Mortality, too, is a bond.

On Meat

As is his custom and his pleasure, my Colombian son-in-law tucks into his steak—*la carne* in Spanish and *carne* in Italian, echoing the Latin *carn-* or *caro* (flesh), as do carnal in English (having a relation to the body as opposed to the soul), carnival (a time of feasting and fleshly indulgence as opposed to Lent and fasting), carnivorous and carnivore (flesh-eating animals, as opposed to herbivorous and herbivore, plant eaters). Among flora, the carnation is a flower as red as raw meat, as blood.

Meathead suggests more muscle than brains. Sexual organs are called meat. Males are said to beat their meat. Women are objectified as pieces of meat (Antony even calls Cleopatra cold leftovers on dead Caesar's trencher). Philip Roth's Portnoy actually gets off inside a piece of liver (http://www.npr.org/templates/story/story.php?storyId=88787165).

Venery refers both to deer hunting and to sex, as in venereal disease, Venus, and venison. "My dear" could be "my deer." Horny refers to stags and stag parties. Both hunters and lovers have trysts, or secret meetings. The hunter's tryst is the camouflaged platform where he waits to shoot his arrow at the unsuspecting deer. The lovers' is the bedroom, as in *Gawain and the Green Knight,* where both trysts are simultaneous and parallel: the lady of the castle hunts Gawain's chastity as her lord hunts deer:

> … Thus frollicked the lord on the fringe of the forest,
> And Gawain the good in his gay bed reposed…,
> As softly he slumbered, a slight sound he heard
> … The lady it was, most lovely to look at,
> Who shut the door after her stealthily, slyly,
> And turned toward the bed …

Benjamin Franklin struggled with Chastity in his schedule of self-improvement: "Rarely use Venery except for Health or Offspring;

Never to Dullness, Weakness, or the Injury of your own or another's Peace or Reputation."

St. Augustine confessed: "I love a kind of light, and melody, and fragrance, and meat, and embracement when I love my God, the light, melody, fragrance, meat, embracement of my inner man: where there shineth unto my soul what space cannot contain, and there soundeth what time beareth not away, and there smelleth what breathing disperseth not, and there tasteth what eating diminisheth not, and there clingeth what satiety divorceth not" (Book IX).

No creatures on Noah's ark ate each other, and after the Great Flood, God promised Noah's descendants "Every moving thing that liveth shall be meat for you."

Of course, for observant Catholics, no meat on Fridays.

In his later, religious years, Tolstoy preached against eating meat. He gave up hunting, visited and described slaughter houses, questioned butchers, and was horrified by the killing. He claimed that consuming meat "only serves to develop animal feelings, to excite desire, and to promote fornication and drunkenness. And this is continually being confirmed by the fact that young, kind, un-depraved people … without knowing how it logically follows, feel that virtue is incompatible with beefsteaks, and, as soon as they wish to be good, give up eating flesh" (http://www.animal-rights-library.com/texts-c/tolstoy01.htm).

On a school trip to the Plymouth Plantation, my then-eight-year-old daughter witnessed a Pilgrim chop off a turkey's head, and refused to eat meat for many years afterwards.

I came from a meat-eating family. When we went out to eat, we each ordered roast beef au jus. My mother served roast lamb and beef, steak (on special occasions tenderloin, which, she said "melted like butter in your mouth"), lamb chops, meatloaf, ham, turkey and

95

chicken. We rarely ate fish. My oldest brother was a hunter, and once when he shot a stag, he brought it home and left it with Howard, our neighborhood butcher, to carve up and store in his freezer. But when we tried his venison for dinner, Mom and Dad decided it was too tough and "racy" tasting, and the rest was thrown out.

(By coincidence, my father was assigned *Alcohol—One Man's Meat,* by Edward A. Strecker around this time as part of his treatment for alcoholism.)

Meat means substance ("the meat of the argument") as well as sustenance ("where's the beef?").

As a grad student in the 1960s, I cooked for myself in the rooming-house kitchen and shopped at a corner market nearby, where the owner, Sol Levine, who was also the butcher, took a kindly interest in me. He asked why I chose the expensive milk? Buy the other one, you want to save money, don'tcha? Same milk, no difference. So I retrieved the other. Moved by his own good deed, So there you are, he said; go back and get busy and happy. I responded, Being busy isn't always being happy, which struck a chord. He said, "Oh, don't you worry, it'll come around. You'll be eatin' filet mignon in a little while." For the next five years, Sol kept me in prime cut meats, which he'd save for me without charging full price, whether for roasts or for hamburger, which he ground fresh while we talked. He told me about his life, sometimes for hours, leaning against his meat case. Shortly before we met, he'd been widowed after forty-four years of marriage. He had a son and two daughters and five grandchildren. He was 73. He'd already distributed his estate, so there would be no quarreling after he was gone. He was working for free for his son and daughter-in-law in the store; they had the upstairs apartment and he lived in back. He told me he was up before dawn to drive his van to the North End and get the best sides wholesale. He shared and tried to teach me not only about grades of meat but also about the meat of life. He'd lost most of his family to the Holocaust, but his mother had survived, and when she reached New York, she had held and kissed him so hard he worried she'd left a hole in his cheek.

I stopped eating meat in mid-life more out of curiosity than conscience. I had discovered distance running and was surrounded by vegetarian friends and coworkers in my teaching (my daughter had reverted to meat when she came of age). How did vegetarians manage? What did they eat? Cheese, bagels, pasta, fruits, nuts, and vegetables, milk, eggs, yogurt? I acquired new tastes. I lost weight. I felt clearer, emotionally and intellectually. My wife supported me. My doctor approved. I never had meat dreams. I enjoyed a certain righteousness, and due exception. At catered school events, I asked for vegetarian options. Likewise, at restaurants and dinner parties, including Thanksgiving with family friends.

A full decade later without meat, I started slipping. Why not hard salami? Why not real bacon occasionally? Why not sausage patties? Why not compromise when there was no veg option? Eat the ham or barbecue out of good manners? I was now a "mostly vegetarian," my wife said. I'd never been serious on principle anyway. She seemed complicit and relieved.

As for my son-in-law, he's lean, works hard, and craves red meat as a way of remaining true to his culture. I eat mostly turkey, as if that is healthier somehow. Turkey burgers, turkey ham, turkey bacon, turkey meat balls. And as for Tolstoy's logic, I live with the guilt, but also with realism, self-acceptance, and deliberate stupidity. I don't dwell on the evil, nor on my animal brothers with spiritual regard. Animists, I read, thank the animals they kill: "When a large animal is killed or a large fish is caught, the hunter or fisherman may cry over its death to appease the animal spirit. Hunters also apologize to animals when they are killed, saying that they needed to take the meat and hide for their survival" (http://buryatmongol.org/a-course-in-mongolian-shamanism/the-natural-world/spirits-of-animals-totems-animal-guides-and-hunting/). It is to think too curiously, I think, to trace my styrofoam tray of red hamburger sealed in plastic wrap forever fresh and waiting in the supermarket (no butcher or meat cutter in sight) back to the refrigerated boxcar and truck, the meat processing plant, the slaughterhouse, the stockyard and feeding pens, the crowded cattle truck, the herd and range, the individual creature. It's just meat. And though I do (I do!) weep at the stories of a farm kid given a lamb to raise as a pet, giving it a name, then one day having to surrender it for slaughter and eat its flesh; or, similarly cheer for the preservation of Wilbur as Some Pig, I also understand the need of being versed in country things.

At some level, to live is to kill. We're both hunters and gatherers. We wield tools in place of fangs. We dream of paradise, where we feed in innocence; and our worst nightmare, even worse than the Donner Party, or Dante's Ugolino—"And then the hunger had more / Power than even sorrow over me" (Canto XXXIII, ln. 70–73), is Soylent Green: "Next thing, they'll be breeding us like cattle, for food." (https://www.youtube.com/watch?v=6zAFA-hamZ0).

In India, sacred cows wander among the starving poor.

On Empathy

Wary of the verb "empathize"—together with its noun "empathy" and adjective "empathic"—I probably use "identify with," "feel with," or "relate to" instead. I know that empathy and sympathy are often confused (and share a common Greek root in pathos or feeling, especially in response to suffering). The usual distinction is between feeling *with* and feeling *for*. "Compassion," to feel together, is a synonym for both; while "pity" sounds patronizing compared to either. And without the "sym-," which means "similar," "pathetic" sounds scornful.

We send sympathy rather than empathy cards to the bereaved, for instance. Not only is writing a letter and finding the right words difficult, but to some degree impertinent. We want the bereaved to know that they're not alone, and that we are aware of their pain, but at the same time don't want to intrude on it. The cards speak for us, and are personalized by our signature. "Heartfelt sympathy," they say. "Warm Thoughts ... Condolences during this difficult time ... I feel for you, I'm thinking of you, and I'd do anything to help.... I could not possibly understand what you are feeling.... I want to send my deepest sympathy.... I'm willing to listen.... Sorry for your loss."

D.H. Lawrence criticized Walt Whitman's sympathy: "Eskimos are not minor little Walts. They are something I am not. I know that.... He does not say love. He says sympathy. Feeling with. Feel with them as they feel with themselves.... He [confounds] it with Jesus's Love and Paul's Charity...." If Lawrence isn't confused here, I am. By "sympathy" Whitman must mean empathy. Or perhaps Lawrence objects to Walt's sentimentality—Walt's feelings for the "other" are driven by idealism, and exaggerated, if not affected.

The opposite of feeling for or with is indifference, or worse, antipathy. You're so vain you prob'ly think this song is about you. In large cities, the likelihood of acts of random meanness is higher than that of kindness. We don't want to get involved, we say. We're defensive, if not self-absorbed. We ignore the homeless, and even the injured. George Eliot's rural observation (in *Middlemarch*) seems like our excuse: "If we had a keen vision and feeling for all ordinary human life, it would be like hearing the grass grow and the squirrel's heart beat, and we should die of that roar which lies on the other side of silence. As it is, the quickest of us walk about well wadded with stupidity."

Some of us have more imagination than others, of course, particularly writers. Some of us are more capacious and generous. We can bear more or less pain. Thom Jones's great story, "I Want to Live," is his imagining of his mother-in-law's decline with terminal cancer: "Where was the *empathy?*" she thinks about her doctor. "Why did he get into this field if he couldn't empathize? In this field, empathy should be your stock-in-trade." Her son-in-law (the writer), on the other hand, cheers her. He advocates for methadone and finds temporary remedies for side-effects. "The son-in-law understood. Of all the people to come through. It's bad and it gets worse and so on until the worst of all.... 'What does it feel like?'" he asks her. "'... Like that? Really? Jittery! Oh, God, that must be awful.... I couldn't—I'd take a bottle of pills, shoot myself.... I know I couldn't handle chemo.'" He reads and shares Schopenhauer. He helps with unfinished business. He's genuine company.

Just as a preoccupation with physical fitness has spread from gyms to the general culture, the practice of mindfulness has spread from ashram to PBS and seeks to develop empathy in a world where technology threatens to isolate and distract us. "In the U.S. in recent years, mindfulness meditation has become a mainstream stress reducer, widely practiced in schools, corporations, and even by a Member of Congress" (http://www.pbs.org/video/religion-and-ethics-newsweekly-mindfulness-going-mainstream/). "Meditation increases compassionate responses to suffering," argue researchers in *Psychological Science* 24 (10). Memoirist Beth Kephart has recently proposed that each town should organize an

Empathy Project, where locals meet and listen to each other (http://www.philly.com/philly/opinion/commentary/finding-empathy-in-a-time-of-division-20170607.html). In self-awareness begins awareness of others, supposedly.

When it comes to differences, E.M. Forster's word, "tolerance," isn't enough. During WWII, he asks what we can do with defeated Nazis. "Tolerance means putting up with people, being able to stand things.... This is the only force which will enable different races and classes and interests to settle down together to the work of reconstruction.... There are two solutions. One of them is the Nazi solution. If you don't like people, kill them.... The other way.... is on the whole the way of the democracies.... If you don't like people, put up with them as well as you can. Don't try to love them, you can't, you'll only strain yourself. But try to tolerate them.... Tolerance carries on when love gives out.... It's dull. And yet it entails imagination." Of course later, in his *Aspects of the Novel* lectures, Forster argues that "We cannot understand each other, except in a rough and ready way; we cannot reveal ourselves, even when we want to; what we call intimacy is only a makeshift; perfect knowledge is an illusion."

Considerate doesn't mean empathic, though empathic people are likely to be considerate. Considerate means being respectful of the rights of others and their privacy, space, and freedoms. We make allowances for a late night party down the street, at least at first, but as it grows rowdier, we call the cops. The partiers themselves don't consider us. They're disturbing the peace.

President Obama insisted on "empathy" as a requirement for his Supreme Court nominees. A woman on the court, he argued, would temper justice with mercy and protect progressive social reforms: "we need somebody who's got the heart—the empathy—to recognize what it's like to be a young teenage mom. The empathy to understand what it's like to be poor or African-American or gay or disabled or old—and that's the criteria by which I'll be selecting my judges" (2007).

Conservative jurists were offended by the idea that legal objectivity was a myth, and that white male bias could only be balanced by other biases, as determined by different backgrounds and experiences.

Think of the powerless Lear, more sinned against than sinning, discovering first sympathy: "Take physic, pomp, / Expose thyself to feel what wretches feel"; then reasoning in madness against all mortal judgment: "The usurer hangs the cozener.… None does offend, I say, none." Well, yes and no. Evil still prevails, at least until the offenders destroy each other (together with Cordelia).

"How would you feel if someone did that to you?" we ask our children; and then apologize while punishing them: "This hurts me more than it hurts you."

Contemporary psychologists disagree about what empathy is, and whether it is for good or for ill. If good, it may improve morality and relatedness in a world of "absurd" suffering; if ill, it may add to the suffering. In *Against Empathy: the case for rational compassion* (2016), Paul Bloom rejects emotional empathy as "a poor moral guide," one that favors the few over the many and "can lead to irrational and unfair political decisions…; can corrode certain important relationships, such as between a doctor and patient, and make us worse at being friends, parents, husbands and wives." For truer kindness, he instead recommends self-control and intelligence, which make for a "more diffuse compassion." However, other psychologists contest his separation of the emotional and cognitive, and argue that one leads naturally to the other. They are connected. "It is our ability to generalize and to direct our empathy through the use of reason that is our saving grace," write Drs. Denise and Robert Cummins. "Without that, it is easy to create a holocaust, a crusade, or a jihad" (https://www.psychologytoday.com/blog/good-thinking/201310/why-paul-bloom-is-wrong-about-empathy-and-morality).

Meanwhile, surrounded and blessed by larger hearts than my own, I wonder if I suffer from "empathy deficiency disorder," a term coined by

Douglas LaBier Ph.D., director, Center for Progressive Development (https://www.psychologytoday.com/blog/the-new-resilience/201004/ are-you-suffering-empathy-deficit-disorder). Empathy is hard-wired in all of us, he explains, but the more we are conditioned by our materialistic society, the more we equate status, money, and power with who we are. "EDD keeps you locked inside a self-centered world." We can, however, develop more empathy through mental exercise. At odds with your wife? Consider some aspect that your partner dislikes about you, then "shift your consciousness into your partner's perspective"; try to "understand rather than to judge." With enemies, and with strangers, as well; think how or why they are hostile, allow for your own mistakes, "open yourself to seeing yourself through their eyes"; with those different from you, allow for the commonalities, such as hopes, dreams, and disappointments. The "mirror neurons" will fire.

Nevertheless I need to guard against pain, intrusion, sentimentality, self-congratulation, and preaching. I protect myself in order to function, I tell myself. Unlike my wife, I hang up on charity calls. I feel squeamish and reluctant to visit my dying brother six hours away. It's usually my wife who feels and insists on the decent thing, instinctive where I am defensive (and once she does convince me to go, afterwards I'm glad). When a campus rival, who was struggling with cancer, accused me of coldness in opposing his promotion, he was right. Even before being sick, he had failed to publish; and as for compassion, he had family for that. When family friends lost their 9-year-old son, I felt their suffocating pathos, but also felt glad for my own son's health. Their bad luck, I thought. On the other hand, I grieved with my distant sister and her 34-year-old son, a painter, as he declined from AIDS: "In missing, or in getting ready to miss you, what I feel, John, is a debt," I wrote to him. Later I edited *Sorrow's Company: Writers on Loss and Grief*, an anthology of "writing [that] reminds me to value the living ... and never, ever to take a person, friend, lover, daughter, son, neighbor, colleague, student, for granted, though in living I must."

I respond to uncommon kinships: those whom I admit to my soul's society. The compassion I feel for the victims of natural disasters, on the other hand, is more abstract, like the radio announcer's, who on witnessing the *Hindenburg* explode, gasped, "Ah, the humanity!" The victims' claim is on our common nature, where no one is more valuable than another.

As soldiers, we "turn off the switch inside our head" (says Tim O'Brien about combat in Vietnam). We practice necessary numbness; and dehumanizing the enemy, are ourselves dehumanized. Life is cheap.

I'm quick to condemn everyday jerks (see https://aeon.co/essays/so-you-re-surrounded-by-idiots-guess-who-the-real-jerk-is and http://www.nytimes.com/2007/01/18/fashion/18difficult.html), for being dense, overweening, humorless, and sick of self-love: all traits I fear and despise as my own. Jerks try my patience, if not my empathy, since they lack both. They seem like obstacles to a better world.

*

Close-hearted; empty-hearted; open-hearted.

*

Tell a story, I tell my students, about someone of different gender, race, class, age, body type, occupation, and/or values. You'll need to pay attention. Question, listen, and observe; read authors from these groups. Even if you start with prejudice, story-telling demands due regard. Take Andre Dubus's story "Fat Girl," for instance, and his risk of offending readers who are sensitive about body image and gender.

*

Caveat: hucksters and seducers use their understanding to exploit us. They prey on our weaknesses. They recognize our commonality, but leave the switch off. At once empathic and predatory, they want our money, touch, or vote.

*

Reading and writing stories may inspire compassion, but mainly while we're doing them, or in their afterglow, which fades. Dostoyevski can give me a temporary psychological high; D.H. Lawrence a sense of "blood knowledge." Sherwood Anderson hoped that his stories would "[break] down a little the curious separateness of so much of life." I recall an eminent male professor's introducing Tillie Olsen by crediting "Tell Me A Riddle" with making him kinder to his wife.

*

We must feel and not feel, it seems to me. We learn to relinquish those we love. We brace, if not harden our hearts. Parents let their children go; and children their parents. Both cruel and kind, we leave as we are left, though we keep in touch and ready to help. Of course, "past hope is past care," is one common saying, yet "where there's life, there's hope" is equally true.

*

We have call to believe in progress, both personal and cultural. Steven Pinker's *The Better Angels of Our Nature* argues that the humanitarian revolution of the eighteenth century led to lasting reforms and to our present demand for world-wide human rights. Not that empathy exists only in and between humans. Dogs show it towards each other and their masters, and we feel it for animals even as we "put them out of their misery." Surely, the world would be happier with more compassion, and Roman Krananc sees it as "a most valuable and valued twenty-first-century asset" (https://www.salon.com/2014/11/08/the_one_thing_that_could_save_the_world_why_we_need_empathy_now_more_than_ever/), though endangered. A University of Michigan study found in 2011 "that college students today scored 40% lower in empathy than those of the past decades, with the biggest drop coming at the turn of the millenium" (http://newsinfo.inquirer.net/445421/lack-of-empathy-in-a-wired-world), suggesting that while connecting and informing us the internet and social media also serve to distract and stunt feeling (http://rhettsmith.com/2010/06/college-students-and-empathy-can-social-media-create-a-bystander-effect-that-can-inhibit-ones-compassion/). As products of the wired world, millenials are conditioned (or so goes the argument) to superficial thinking and relationships. They surf and globe trek. Are locked into private portals of chat and entertainment and zoned out of family discussions. Media violence makes them "insensitive to others' pain." They are "hypercompetitive and expectant," etc., etc. If so, then neural calesthentics need to reverse the trend: therapy, medication, mediation, different educational styles, art, and religion. Survival is at stake. Personhood and destiny. Or maybe not.

What rough beast slouches towards Bethlehem?

Even wondering helps.

On Color

My wife's summer garden is to the eye as music to the ear. Ear registers different wavelengths of sound, the eye of light. The pleasures are in the blendings, contrasts, symmetries; and, curiously in our perception's motion. Painters know this. We read paintings as they invite the eye, as shape and color combine, left to right, up, down. The motion is ours, our eyeballs turn and irises adjust, sweeping, rolling, searching for rhythms.

Monochrome, we say. One color. Black on white. Grayscale. Brown on white. Sepia. And then Technicolor. The sepia door opens onto Munchkinland. The startle, deliberately garish, of sudden primary colors in a land of dream and wonder: vivid reds, greens, yellows, blues. Ruby slippers! Yellow brick road! Horse of a different color! On my first flight from wintry Boston to Cartagena, Columbia, I felt that way. Vivid, blazing colors everywhere, not only in the tropical flora/fauna (exotic birds!), but in the painted buildings, in the clothes and cars.

Of course in my dreams, or even when I shut my eyes, I can recall no colors, despite researchers reporting that most people do dream in color, or think they do.

Different substances reflect light in different wave lengths, the wave lengths stimulate cells in the human retina—some 120 million rods and 6 or 7 million cones. Hence with fall foliage in New England; as the leaf turns molecularly from alive to dead, it turns from reflecting light in the green range of 450–560 nanometers to that in the yellow, orange and red range of 560–700 nanometers (https://www.fs.fed.us/fallcolors/2013/science.shtml). At twilight or eclipse: "brightness falls from the air." There are no colors at night, except in artificial light (see Edward Hopper's paintings). A grey day. All colors tinted, muted, bland. But at night, in street or headlight or flashlight's shine, they seem surprised and not themselves. A peony in moonlight.

Blind Milton (formerly sighted) describes Satan's hell at first sight as "waste and wild … yet from those flames / No light; but rather darkness visible" (*Paradise Lost,* I, 62-64), and later as Poet laments that "Not with me / Returns the day, or sweet approach of even or morn,/ Or sight of vernal bloom, or summer's rose … or human face divine. / But cloud instead and ever-during dark," and prays for Celestial Light to "Shine inward … that I may see and tell / Of things invisible to mortal sight" (*PL,* II, 21–27).

Where humans have three kinds of cone cells, responding to three bands of light (red, green, blue), other species have more kinds and can see ultraviolet wavelengths we cannot, just as dogs's ears pick up high-pitched sounds. On the other hand, cats and owls have night vision because they have more rod receptors than we do, rather than cones. We, of course, have developed night-vision goggles that either enhance dim light, send out infrared beams and read their reflections, or read the heat energy that objects themselves emit. Heat-imaging instruments aboard a helicopter detect a fugitive bomber hiding in a backyard boat. The images are tinted green (https://electronics. howstuffworks.com/gadgets/high-tech-gadgets/nightvision.htm). Elsewhere, researchers hope that the blind can learn to detect infrared wavelengths with their tongues, and thereby see the world in terms of heat variations (https://www.scientificamerican.com/article/device-lets-blind-see-with-tongues/).

In 1667, one year after *Paradise Lost* was published, Sir Isaac Newton discovered the visible color spectrum. Shining sunlight through a prism, he projected seven different colors: Red, Orange, Yellow, Green, Blue, Indigo and Violet. He also found that when the bands of color were passed through another, inverted prism they emerged as white light; also that when only one ray passed though a prism it retained its color. He diagrammed the basic colors in a circle or wheel, relating their complements, contrasts, and gradations. But where Newton considered colors a property of light, Goethe in 1810 considered them a "feature of our perception of the world" (https://library.si.edu/exhibition/

color-in-a-new-light/science). Goethe modified Newton's color wheel, linked colors to personality types, and influenced nineteenth-century artists. Yet today's color wheel corresponds mostly to Newton's. The primary colors, red, yellow, and blue mix to create secondary colors, with tint and hue determined by additions of white or black, and primaries and secondaries blend to create tertiaries, such as blue-green or turquoise (https://en.wikipedia.org/wiki/Color_wheel).

Children with crayons, pencils, or water colors quickly learn that red and blue make purple, yellow and blue make green, etc. We tell them that white comes from mixing the primary colors together, though it never seems to work. And black, supposedly "the absence of color," is an outlier, a crayon, pencil, or ink all its own. At 3 or 4, my granddaughter colored before she could draw, so I drew outlines for her in ballpoint, and she colored them in, grass, sky, clouds, tree trunk, leaves, flowers, her colors enlivening even my inept sketches.

Greek and Roman sculptures were originally colorized, reports Matthew Gurewitsch in Smithsonian magazine: "[The Greeks] ... thought of their gods in living color and portrayed them that way too. The temples that housed them were in color, also, like mighty stage sets. Time and weather have stripped most of the hues away. And for centuries people who should have known better pretended that color scarcely mattered" (http://www.smithsonianmag.com/arts-culture/true-colors-17888/#rEA8mVX8FmpjgHIZ.99). However, Vinzenz Brinkmann, a German archaeologist, having revealed pigment residues on the original works under ultra-violent light, has matched the ancient compounds and hand-painted plaster and marble replicas. "Vitality is what the Greeks were after," Brinkmann says about the Cuirass-Torso from the Acropolis, "that, and the charge of the erotic.... Dressing this torso and giving it color was a way to make the body sexier."

Show your true colors, we say, meaning your authentic values and nature, which we disguise for various reasons. Chameleons change color as a defense mechanism. We use camouflage to blend soldiers and equipment into the landscape, so they won't be detected and targeted. One's "colors" are also the flag or nation for which they fight. Instance the pirate ship, lowering its British flag and flying the Jolly Roger.

My wife still colors her hair, presumably to look younger in our agist culture. I colored my own for several years, feeling that remaining brown helped me to fit in better with students and colleagues. But then I stopped, wearied of my own vanity. I remember, too, meeting an African-American businessman decades before (we'd both been in our late twenties), and his boasting that he dyed his hair with streaks of white, so his clients, workers and family would respect him as wise. Now my students dye their hair from brown, black, red, or blonde to green tips, blue, vermillion: "unnatural" colors on purpose.

The peacock's tail fans full and iridescent to bedazzle peahens. Likewise most male birds are more colorful than females, perhaps because the females prefer "bright colors in males," or because dull colors protect females, "while incubating," from predators. Colors help birds to recognize their kind, to warn off predators, and between males signal that a mate and territory are taken and "the occupant is in good condition and prepared to fight" (https://www.scientificamerican. com/article/why-are-male-birds-more-c/).

Artists, designers, psychologists, and psychics link colors to emotion. There are hot colors and cold. Red "radiates pure energy and increases the pulse rate," yellow "stimulates mental activity," blue is calm and stable, and soothes pain, green recalls nature and money. For those who claim to see auras, red indicates an adventurous spirit, yellow an analytic one, pink a generous and healing, black a hateful, etc. Painters use color to create a 3-D illusion on the 2-D canvas: red appears to advance, blue to recede.

Following Goethe's theory of perception, Impressionists and Post-Impressionists freed color as an "intrinsic property of objects" and painted emotion using "non-naturalistic colors and forms". Hence a green face, a red studio, a blue man, and eventually a cubist nude descending the staircase. They explored how colors from either side of the color wheel combine to please the eye, but clash with their opposite; how the attributes of color are determined by the amount of red and green or of blue and yellow; how any color will "cast a shadow" tinged with its opposite; and how each is "more distinctly seen when next to its contrary" (www.webexhibits.org/colorart/index2.html).

In prose, Flaubert conveys Charles' infatuated vision of Emma Bovary much as a portrait by Renoir: "The parasol, of dove-grey, iridescent silk, with the sun shining through it, cast moving glimmers of light over the white skin of her face. She was smiling beneath it in the mild warmth; and they could hear the drops of water, one by one, falling over the taut moiré." And Hemingway spoke of his "Big Two-Hearted River," as an attempt "to do the landscape in the manner of Cezanne."

Still photography, starting in 1839, seemed purely representational. We have Mathew Brady's daguerreotypes of the Civil War and of Lincoln; however, color experiments began with Andrew Levy in 1851, and Gabriel Lippmann in 1886 was the first to produce a color photograph "without the aid of any pigments or dyes," for which he won the Nobel in Physics in 1906. Color film and cameras became widely available in the 1920s. As a boy, I developed black-and-white snapshots at home, but had to send away exposed color film for processing either as slides or prints. Self-developing color Polaroids began in the late 1950s. And since the 1990s, digital photography has replaced analogue. Full-color selfies abound.

Not all color is reflected light. There is translucence, as with filters, stained-glass windows, color slides or glowing canopies of leaves. There are *incandescence* (Edison's lightbulb), *chemiluminescence,* and *fluorescence* or *phosphorescence.* Think of city lights: neon signs, LCD billboards and TVs, strings of holiday lights, ballpark arc lights, search lights, the flashing lights of emergency vehicles. My LCD backlit computer screen, and its 227 pixels per square inch.

Milton Glaser's poster of Bob Dylan's mental rainbow prefigures MRI images of orgasms in the brain, beginning with red and flooding with yellow and white as synapses fire and oxygen levels change (https://jezebel.com/5859785/watch-the-worlds-first-movie-of-the-female-brain-during-orgasm).

Colorful language means rich in metaphor and emotion, though an off-color remark is one considered earthy and crude. By contrast, language is colorless when bland and denotative. Attitudes and feelings *color* our judgments and perceptions. In blue light, red paint appears black. Black light causes minerals to fluoresce (hence fluorescent body paint).

In "The Investment," Robert Frost speculates about a backwoods couple, who have suddenly painted their house and bought a piano to "get some music and color out of life."

My parents and I visited my oldest brother, who had settled in Colorado ("colored red"). He'd written home about the aspens in the mountains turning such bright colors that they were mistaken for forest fires. My mother ohhed and ahhed at the spectacular sunsets from Ft. Collins, while I busily took color slides, though they could never suggest the full beauty: the immensity of space, the eastern hemisphere of dark, then twilight closing overhead while perhaps a third of the sky remained bright over the mountains, yet softened, the sinking sun burned and the horizon was streaked with reds, oranges, turquoise and lavender, with deeper purple in the clouds.

Years before, near home back East, she'd been painting a covered bridge while I played with stones on a sandbar. when she exclaimed of another sunset: "No one would believe a sky like that even if I could paint it; it doesn't matter if it's true, no one would believe it." I think now both of the pretend statue in *The Winter's Tale:* "O, she's warm! / If this be magic, let it be an art / Lawful as eating," and Johnson's dictum, "Imitations are not to be mistaken for reality, but to bring reality to mind."

Fireworks, the burst and bloom of colored sparks fill the sky.

Green vegetables: beans, celery, broccoli, and lettuce. Yellow corn, squash, pears, lemons, grapefruits, and bananas. Orange pumpkins, carrots, and oranges. Peppers and apples both in red, yellow, and green. Potatoes tan. Supposedly the produce displays in supermarkets need "high color definition lamps," according to one manufacturer. "Strawberries and radishes tend to look dull, leafy lettuce wilts, bananas and oranges go soft and mushy and cauliflower turns yellow under common supermarket lighting" (http://www.promolux.com/english/retail_produce.php).

Caught red-handed (think of Macbeth's bloody hands, which would "incarnadine" the sea). Red-faced with shame. Green with envy. Greenhorn. True blue. Blue in the face. In the pink. Yellow livered. Feeling blue. The mean reds. White as a ghost. Fiery red (blue flame is hottest, of course, yellow least). Red hot. Sky blue. Canary yellow. Golden light. Avocado green. Green eyes. Blue. Hazel. Brown. Skin pigments: red, yellow, tan, brown, white (pink), and shades thereof. The rainbow coalition. The rainbow connection.

Do we over-privilege the vivid, I wonder, as we do the loud, spicy, strong, and pungent? The Pantone book boasts 2,310 values and shades: an orchestra, a symphony! We are the nexus of our senses, dwelling in the world and—thanks to NASA's spectroscopy and other instruments—the universe they define.

As for our garden, it's more like a jazz quartet. Against a backdrop of greens, from simple (marigolds, tulips, coreopsis, poppies) to complex colors (columbines, irises), the blaze of petals and pollen centers, each bloom a clarion of smell, shape and color to attract the hairy-legged bees, who pollinate with dust from other blooms and trigger seed. The floral world's congress and dance.

On Blood

If we think of warm, red blood as a sign of humanity, in fact all vertebrate/mammalian blood is red. Hematologists explain that red "comes from the hemoglobin used by red blood cells in the transport of oxygen, which has an atom of iron as the receptor for the charge the oxygen is on." Cold, non-vertebrate blood can be other colors: crabs, for instance, have green blood (thanks to their using copper "as the receptor element"); the Antarctic octopus has blue, and various insects have clear, yellow, or green blood (https://news.nationalgeographic. com/2015/03/150312-blood-antarctica-octopus-animals-science-colors/).

In any case, sharks get frenzied by ours, and mosquitoes, ticks, lice, and now vampire bats feed on it (http://www.telegraph.co.uk/science/2017/01/13/vampire-bats-have-caught-sucking-human-blood-first-time/).

We have about 5.3 quarts in our adult bodies, and can "bleed out" from wounds. Most cuts are closed by coagulation, sometimes helped by compresses, dressings, and stitches. By "warm-blooded person," we mean alive; although psychopaths, as Truman Capote wrote, kill "in cold blood." They are seemingly inhuman and unfeeling. "Hot-blooded" refers to passionate, and quick to lust and rage. "A bleeding heart" is sentimental.

Humans have 8 possible blood types, and types (as in "You're not my type") need to be compatible for transfusions. Type O positive is the most common and compatible with all other types except O negative. If blood types don't match, the blood clumps in transfusion, which leads to a heart attack (for all compatibilities, see https://www.redcrossblood.org/donate-blood/how-to-donate/types-of-blood-donations/blood-types.html). The chemistry of clumping was only discovered in the 1900s, in time for World War I. Before that, as early as the 1700s, there were attempted transfusions from animals to humans, and between other, different kinds of animals, which usually led to death. Human-to-human was necessary for serious surgery, yet often failed.

"Early transfusions used whole blood, but modern medical practice commonly uses only components of the blood, such as red blood cells, white blood cells, plasma, clotting factors, and platelets" (https://en.wikipedia.org/wiki/Blood_transfusion). During WWI, the use of anti-coagulants and refrigeration made it possible to store donor blood for several days and to perform "non-direct" transfusions. By WWII, blood plasma served as a substitute for whole blood; liquid plasma was replaced by dried (to be mixed with distilled water as needed), making it easier to store in blood banks and to transport long distances. By the Korean war, plastic bags had replaced bottles for collection, storage, and delivery.

Bloodletting, on the other hand, was a common treatment for nearly all conditions and diseases from ancient times up to the 1900s. The Greeks believed that blood was one of four "humours" (along with phlegm, black bile and yellow bile), that excess or stagnant blood caused disease, and that bleeding would restore "humoral balance." They modeled the process on menstruating, which Hippocrates believed "[purged] women of bad humours." In the nineteenth century, medical bloodletting was practiced by "barber-surgeons," who were announced by their red-and-white-striped barber poles (the red symbolizing blood and the white, bandages). Leeches were also commonly used. "Many sessions would end only when the patient began to swoon." Only in the twentieth century has bloodletting been considered ineffective and "as a general health measure ... proven to be harmful" (https://en.wikipedia.org/wiki/Bloodletting).

"Let us make an incision for your love," says the Moorish prince (in *The Merchant of Venice*), "To prove whose blood is reddest." "Only my blood speaks to you in my veins," protests Bassanio. "If you prick us, do we not bleed?" warns Shylock. "This bond doth give thee here no jot of blood," rules Portia/Balthazar. Blood symbolizes our common humanity, despite social, racial, and cultural differences.

In the Bible, both human and animal bloods are sacred. In sacrifices, "blood was caught by the priest in a basin, and then sprinkled seven times on the altar" (http://www.revelation.co/2009/02/22/what-does-the-bible-say-about-blood/). "Only flesh with its soul—its blood—you must not eat," God tells Noah. (Genesis 9:4). "The soul of every sort of flesh is its blood" (Leviticus 17:14). The custom of hanging butchered animals to drain their meat is related to these beliefs; while eating blood pudding, not to mention rare steak, defies them. Echoing God's testing Abraham in ordering to sacrifice Isaac, God later sacrifices his only son, in Christian belief, and we are "washed in the blood of the lamb," as we receive the sacramental wafer and wine as Christ's body and blood. Mysteries and superstitions. As believers, Jehovah's Witnesses still oppose transfusions.

Though we know now that blood itself has no part in genetics, we nonetheless still refer to bloodlines (royal, noble, common), as if inherited characteristics are passed down by blood, rather than by genomes. We speak of good blood and bad; mixed blood and pure. We say "it's in my blood." We speak of "red-blooded American" (meaning patriotic, courageous, vigorous, and decent). We say of family, tribe, and race, that we "share the same blood," or have "blood ties"; that "blood is thicker than water"; or "my blood runs in your veins"; or "blood tells/shows."

Inherited DNA comes from parental sperm and egg, not blood, though blood (along with saliva, hair, body tissue, bone and teeth) is a source of DNA for testing—"present in white blood cells, but not red blood cells, which lack nuclei" (http://www.biology.arizona.edu/human_bio/problem_sets/DNA_forensics_2/06t.html). Also, nurture shapes us as much as, if not more than nature, and another meaning of "breeding" is upbringing. She is "well-bred," Henry James might say.

Inbreeding risks joining the same recessive genes from both parents and producing genetic damage to their offspring. "The intermarrying of royal families was known to produce hemophilia, birth defects, and deformities" (https://en.wikipedia.org/wiki/Cousin_marriage).

Blood brotherhood is a ritual or gesture between "unconsanguinous" friends: as in Hollywood westerns (see 1950's *Broken Arrow*), cut finger/wrist/forearm pressed to cut finger/wrist/forearm. Blood touches, but isn't mixed, really.

President Obama proudly contested biases of breeding and called himself a "mutt," as are we all, if we consult DNA-assisted genealogy.

The hierarchy of nation, class and "blood" was part of Greek polytheism, beginning with the gods (the humanoid ruling class), humans, and beasts. Gods of both sexes had children with mortals and with animals. The result were demigods, such as Aeneas, and semi-human creatures such as centaurs, satyrs, minotaurs, mermaids, and harpies.

Christian kings later claimed "divine right," and Shakespeare teases aristocratic fears of class hybridity in *The Winter's Tale,* where a truant prince courts an apparent shepherdess, and his father, the king, is duly alarmed and goes to investigate in the disguise of a commoner. Witnessing the shepherdess's grace and beauty first-hand, the king at first seems ready to bless the match as he discusses gardening: "we marry / A gentler scion to the wildest stock, / And make conceive a bark of baser kind / By bud of nobler race. This is an art / Which does mend nature—change it rather—but / The art itself is nature." The irony, of course, is that the shepherdess was a foundling, and at this point remains unaware of her royal heritage or the natural fact that all her "acts are queens." Hierarchy is preserved by the end, although her adopted rural family will be promoted to courtier status, once her true identity is revealed and she marries the prince.

Historically, the urge to decide human evolution, as we have engineered that of animals and plants, has inspired and justified self-serving atrocities. All men are created equal, except for those who believe themselves genetically superior. One civilization degrades another, whether Chinese, Western European, or North African. Euro-American colonists and frontiersmen conduct genocide against Native Americans, regarding them as heathens and savages, while also importing captured African blacks as slaves. Prior to Darwin's *The Descent of Man* (1871), there were influential racist ideologues, but Darwin's examination of strains of man as a species, his idea of "natural selection" (albeit from a common ancestor), and the prediction that "civilized races ... will ... replace the savage races": all contributed to the rise of "eugenics" (actually in America before Germany), and ultimately the Nazi campaign for "racial purification." Pseudoscience supported the Nuremberg laws of 1935, "For Protection of German Blood and Honor." The Nazis exempted Germans with mixed heritage from racial laws if they could prove that "all direct ancestors since 1750 were not Jewish"; otherwise, mixed marriage was outlawed as "blood treason." Also inmates of private and state-operated institutions, such as "prisoners, 'degenerates,' dissidents, people with congenital cognitive and physical disabilities" were either sterilized or euthanized (https://en.wikipedia.org/wiki/Nazi_eugenics). In 1941, "the final solution" of exterminating all Jews and other "subhumans" began with the invasion of Poland and Russia. The Nazis massacred nearly one million Jewish civilians, calling them Bolsheviks and enemy insurgents. The following year, they began arresting and sending Jews from central, western and South East Europe to death camps with gas chambers, where some 5.1 million were "efficiently" killed. "When Himmler addressed senior SS personnel and leading members of the regime ... [in 1943], he used the fate of the Jews as a sort of blood bond to tie the civil and military leadership to the Nazi cause" (https://en.wikipedia.org/wiki/Final_Solution). Himmler also supported Nordic breeding with his *Lebensborn* program (https://en.wikipedia.org/wiki/Lebensborn).

After the Nuremberg war-crime trials, and the founding of the UN, a thorough, scientific rebuttal of racist assumptions was made by UNESCO, in the 1951–67 report, *The Race Question* (http://unesdoc.unesco.org/images/0012/001229/122962eo.pdf). International experts agreed that race was primarily a social construct and there was no genetic hierarchy. "We believe biological differences found amongst human racial groups can in no case justify the views of racial inequality, which have been based on ignorance and prejudice, and that all of the differences which we know can well be disregarded for all ethical human purposes."

I've wondered about the resurgent interest in genealogy reflected by online sites offering DNA kits and research (https://www.ancestry.com/). Likely reasons are listed on one such site: to validate family stories, discover famous relatives, find personal ties to historical events, trace medical conditions, find birth parents, follow religious tenets, preserve family culture, join a heritage society, reconnect with relatives, leave a family legacy to future generations (http://www.genealogyintime.com/articles/why-genealogy-is-important.html). Another impetus may be to discover "new sources of status, such as celebrating the resilience of families that survived generations of poverty or slavery, of the success of families in integrating across racial or national boundaries" (https://en.wikipedia.org/wiki/Genealogy).

America is short on history, of course. While some Americans claim *Mayflower* ancestry, the ancestors of others arrived at Ellis Island and had their names Americanized, and still others arrived as slaves. Each immigrant group has struggled to fit in while preserving their native language and traditions. But we've also shared the frontier notion of life as self-invention; identity as what you do, rather than your pedigree.

My own family tree, as far as my parents knew or cared to know, reached back to my father's grandfather, who immigrated from Northern Ireland (I recall his banded wooden trunk in our attic);

and on my mother's side, to a list scrawled by her father of his 11 siblings on a Missouri farm and to my grandmother's account of being orphaned in Germany and shipped as a girl to Missouri relatives with "a name-tag around her neck." What mattered, we gathered, was that our grandfathers succeeded as resourceful businessmen, and our grandmothers became mothers, ladies, and wives. They had risen in fortune through hard work, talents and stick-to-it-iveness. Their examples as well as their genes were in our blood.

My sister first challenged our WASP ranks by marrying and bearing children to a Swarthmore senior, who was half Dutch and half Indonesian (his father had been the Dutch ambassador to Indonesia, and the family had been imprisoned by the Japanese). My sister also left our Eastern roots and settled in California, where visiting was difficult, but there was less racism. In my turn, the youngest and last to marry, I met Connie in Cambridge. She was from a Jewish family in Miami, and her uncle warned us that as a mixed couple we would be neither "one thing nor the other." Still, we dared to be "both things," respecting and drawing on each other's heritages. Our daughter became a traveler both locally and globally, multicultural not only in her heritage, but in relation to her brother, who was Korean (adopted by us as an infant, after secondary infertility). She had her first daughter by a man of African- and Native American descent, who justified his habit of absenteeism as "cultural"; then she moved as a single mom to Cartagena, Colombia, where she married a student from Bogota and had a second daughter. A few years later, they came to the States and lived with us before finding steady work and moving to an apartment nearby.

Indeed, we feel blessed as family, apart from genes. Through school and college, with friends and relationships, our son has told us he always felt a target of white racism. In college, he interned in Hong Kong; and after, returned with a friend to tour Bali and Thailand, then alone to Seoul—where people took him for Korean, but still he felt American. He's settled now and has found work in New

York, as well as a life partner, who is Korean-American, with her first-generation family nearby. Their children will be fully Korean-American, but also share in our cultural legacy: Jewish, Presbyterian, Scotch-Irish, African-American, Native-American, and Hispanic. The past is prologue.

Where biological kinship isn't wholly unconditional or obliged—"But yet thou art my flesh, my blood, my daughter, / Or rather a disease that's in my flesh," rages Lear at Goneril—we also speak of close friends as being "like family." "Soul-sister, -brother, or -mate," we say.

I rarely watch when a nurse pierces my vein and draws samples from my arm. I look away. "Just a pinch," he or she says.

On Envy

If we view the world as arbitrary, whimsical, or corrupt, then envy is self-righteousness: a cry for fairness, reason, and merit. We deserve our share of looks, talents, success, grades, popularity, privileges, health, youth, wealth and possessions, life style, and taste ("No, no," Charley-the-Tuna, "not good taste, but taste good! Sorry, you're rejected for Chicken-Of-The-Sea."). In families, siblings envy each other. Who comes first? Cain slays Abel.

"A feeling of discontent aroused by desire for the possesions or qualities of another," says Webster's. *Invidia* is envy's Latin root. Invidious. Hateful, hostile. To begrudge or covet ("longing for something to which one has no right"). The Tenth Commandment: "You shall not covet your neighbor's house, wife, or property."

Though jealousy can rise from envy, it's not the same emotion. It's more about fear "of being supplanted ... of losing affection or position." You may covet another man's former wife but then grow jealous, having married her, when she flirts with her ex. No man feels "pregnancy *jealousy*," nor woman "penis *jealousy*"; *envy*, yes. Still, we use the terms interchangably.

In her memoir *Writing Past Dark* (1993), Bonnie Friedman warns, "Envy is a vocational hazard for most writers. It festers in one's mind.... It is a sickness; it is a hunger. It is the self consuming the self...." Her antidote is the work itself. "Always one's work. Not the thinking about it. Not the assessing of it. But the *doing* of it."

Psychologists distinguish between malign and benign envy, between "a sick force" that wishes suffering on the object of envy, and a "positive motivational force" that seeks growth and self-improvement (https://en.wikipedia.org/wiki/Envy). "Dante defined this sin as 'love of one's own good perverted to a desire to deprive other men of theirs'" (http://

www.danteinferno.info/7-deadly-sins.html). Ambition, greed, and avarice are cognates.

"All wishes ... have the same and unvarying meaning," argues W. H. Auden in *The Dyer's Hand.* "'I refuse to be what I am.' A wish, therefore, is either innocent and frivolous, a kind of play, or a serious expression of guilt and despair, a hatred of oneself and every being one holds responsible for oneself." It is only a step from this "self-despair" to seeking revenge.

Malign envy and jealousy meet in Iago, whom Coleridge calls a "motiveless malignity." While Iago claims to be jealous of Othello's supposed adultery with Emilia and preference for Cassio, he is really envious of Othello's reputation and idealism. If Iago is *jealous* of anything, it is of Othello's devotion to Desdemona rather than to him (Branagh plays him that way in Oliver Parker's film). Taking his own genius for granted, he is driven by some sense of inferiority or barrenness as inherent as Othello's race. A. C. Bradley views Iago as tragic (*Shakespearean Tragedy,* "Othello"), and Robert Heilman sees his downfall that of "the spiritual have-not" ("Wit and Witchcraft"). He prefigures Milton's Satan, who would rather rule in hell than serve in heaven, and who turns away from Adam and Eve's bliss "for envy; yet with jealous leer malign."

Mozart's rival, Antonio Salieri, is another variation. In Peter Shaffer's play and film, *Amadeus,* Salieri (memorably played by F. Murray Abraham) wishes he were as gifted as Mozart, and that his music pleased God. He believes he has won his place as court composer as a blessing for his piety. Yet realizing that God has gifted Mozart, who is carnal and impious, Salieri seeks revenge on both God and Mozart for his own mediocrity.

In the eighteenth-century literary world, Alexander Pope is secure in his art, which is his livelihood, yet also exasperated by the scribblers of Grub Street ("May some choice patron bless each gray goose quill!"), who seek his favor, pose as rivals and deserve wit's lash, thereby causing his friend, Dr. Arbuthnot, to caution: "Who breaks a butterfly upon a wheel?"

Robert Greene dismissed his rival Shakepeare as an "upstart crow." In Seamus Heaney's parody of the *Inferno,* "An Afterwards," Heaney's wife accompanies Virgil's and finding Heaney in the Ninth Circle rebukes him for neglecting family for careerism "as some maker gaffes me [Heaney] in the neck." In Richard Yates's "Builders," the struggling young writer, Prentice, is reduced to ghostwriting for a cab driver (hacking for a hackie!); and then, having openly mocked the man's "pathetic delusions" and quit, he later comes, after the collapse of his own marriage and dreams, to envy the cabbie's marriage and persistence. In *Advertisements for Myself,* Norman Mailer complains that William Styron convinced his editor to reject *The Deer Park.* In 1970, Ted Solotaroff criticized Rust Hills's "Red Hot Center" in *Esquire* as a "Red Hot Vacuum": "Such centers ... have since fallen prey to the malaise that afflicts the old avant-garde and the random chills and fevers that afflict the new."

That same year, as a jobless PhD and aspiring writer, I co-founded a literary magazine with other young writers. We called it *Ploughshares,* hoping to turn the swords of aesthetic differences to ploughshares, as it were, and to break new ground. Each issue would be edited by a different writer. About literary and little magazines, I later wrote: "The question is less one of providing sanctuary for an avant-garde than it is of providing adequate access and recognition for a whole new generation of writers remarkable for their diversity of directions, and of posing standards of taste deeper than direction itself."

Where "taste," "talent," and "recognition" tend to separate hobbyist, dabbler, or amateur from professional, especially where money is concerned, Harvard psychologist Ellen J. Langer in *On Becoming an Artist* rejects talent as a myth (and hundreds of MFA programs would seem to agree). What matters are "requisite skills," which can be learned and improved on with practice. Warning against "social comparisons," Langer asserts that "we can learn to do most anything.... *Everybody has an equal talent for everything.*" After all, since "audience appreciation," is only "one part conformity, one part a willingness to engage the stimulus, one part the context in which the work is viewed, one part the mindfulness of the viewer, and finally, of course, some aspect of the work itself...," we're free "to engage in any creative activity," simply "to feel alive and in turn become enlivened." The myth of special gifts shouldn't daunt or diminish us.

The Parable of the Talents (Matthew 25:14-30) suggests otherwise. We are stewards of individual gifts, and need to make the most of them—not for personal gain or pride, but for the world's sake. Milton feels this keenly as he fears that loss of sight will render his Talent useless, but then rededicates himself to "present my true account" ("When I Consider How My Light is Spent"). Talent is sacred. You don't hide your Talent under a bushel. Genius is both a gift and a burden that takes its toll.

As for "social comparisons," who do we allow into the lifeboats of our personal vanity? Some living writers I treasure, teach, and learn from rather than envy; others I compete with for publication, grants, jobs, and recognition, consider my peers or inferiors. Still others I feel are wrong-headed; some I dismiss as shallow and over-rated; some I blame for prostituting their talent, or for pretending to have a talent they lack. Those last, of course, mirror my worst self-doubts. Some days it is as painful to peruse a well-stocked bookstore as it is to endure an open-mic reading or read unsolicited mss. As an editor and teacher, it is also painful to be outgrown; to see former students embraced by publishers as much for age, looks and social identity as for their art. Meanwhile writers as a class remain sad hearts in the supermarket (as Randall Jarrell observed), comparing their ignominy to the celebrity of news, sports, music, and media stars.

George Plimpton, the bon vivant, writer, and literary editor, tried as an ordinary man to play at professional sports, acting, music, and even circus acrobatics, then wrote about his experiences as an anti-hero among the stars. He golfed on the PGA tour; pitched against the National League; sparred with prize fighters; scrimmaged with the Detroit Lions and Baltimore Colts; and trained as a goalie with the Boston Bruins. The pros indulged him as a fan and protected him from injury, the better to have his readers appreciate their skills and lives. He knew his place, out of place; and was never seduced by his own fantasies. When it came to envy, he exploited, rather than belied his mediocrity.

Plimpton recalls Shakespeare's Bottom, who enjoys the favors of Titania as readily as acting any role, rather than the later Malvolio, who is sick of self-love and dreams of taking his revenges. As Diana Ross recently pointed out (http://lithub.com/on-envy-the-internet-and-diana-ross/): "Envy is based on your false belief that the other person possesses something magical that exonerates them from the rules of reality.... Once you realize that problems are an inescapable aspect of reality, envy melts away."

Or does it? Think of Richard Yates's Laurel Players ("from the very beginning they had been afraid they would end by making fools of themselves, and they had compounded that fear by being afraid to admit it") and of April Wheeler ("there were hopeful nudges and whispers of 'She's *good*,' and there were stately nods of pride among the several people who happened to know that she had attended one of the leading dramatic schools of New York"), who has some talent, but not enough. Hell is Ted Mack's *Original Amateur Hour, The Gong Show,* or *American Idol.*

Of course, in the '80s, in addition to the magazine, I devoted myself to "audience development." I worked with 225 town libraries to feature local authors, and with the *Boston Phoenix* to hold small press and literary magazine book fairs. We had benefit readings that featured prominent writers, drew audiences of 1000, and promoted an idea of "public publishing." Smaller reading series flourished as well, ranging from discerning venues with audiences of thirty to indiscriminate open mics, where all talents were welcome and the audience was a handful of other writers awaiting their turns. I prided myself on helping to make Boston more receptive to writers, though Yates himself, who had been my mentor at the Iowa Workshop, and who later moved here, warned against squandering my talent on editing, teaching, and organizing instead of finishing my first novel. I had a martyr complex, he said; but I never felt I had a choice.

Presumption. Arrogance. Pride. Contempt. Scorn. Ridicule. Rivalry. Superiority. Inferiority. Pretender. Poseur. Snob. Elitist. Populist. Careerist. Con man. "You are idle, shallow things. I'm not of your element."

The real thing. She has what it takes. He's a natural. No false notes. She's "beyond envy."

Those who seem unable to tell stories, says Leonard Michaels (in a 1986 *Ploughshares*), "refuse to care enough, or fear generosity, or self-revelation, or misinterpretation, or intimacy."

We overcome envy, if we do, with self-awareness, irony, and largesse. "What poor duty cannot do, noble respect / Takes it in might, not merit," proclaims Theseus in selecting the tradesmen's performance. Later, in *Twelfth Night,* Countess Olivia advises Malvolio: "To be generous, guiltless and of a free disposition," and to learn to laugh at himself. ("His secret wish is to violate decorum himself, then relish to its full its power over others," writes C. L. Barber. "No wonder he has not a free disposition when he has such imaginations to keep under!")

Rebecca Frumkin enjoyed collegiality with fellow MFA students: "It was with them that I transcended my smallness and stumbled upon something like generosity of spirit"; nevertheless, back home alone, she "felt so envious of certain people I actually wanted to die" (https://catapult.co/stories/on-envy-the-mfa-and-writing-under-capitalism). Robin Black, in mid-career, has "never met a writer who doesn't envy other writers," and is "amazed at how very little one's achievements do to protect one from the sort of envy … that is painful." She recommends "forcing oneself to be gracious" (http://www.thereviewreview.net/publishing-tips/green-eyed-writer-literary-envy). Kathryn Chetkovich, however, must resign herself to envying her celebrated novelist partner: "I have met the circumstances that are larger than my capacity to be gracious, it turns out. I have come up against the limits of my goodness: someone I love has what I want, and he probably always will. What else is there to do for it? I might as well work" (https://www.theguardian.com/books/2003/jun/22/extract).

What matters is the work.

Writing well—in those moments of luck, grace, and "actualization"—we lose ourselves in the magic; similarly, as readers, we are liberated by the spell of art. It can be done. And when it is, unquestionably, by ourselves and others, we celebrate. The triumph isn't personal. No one is diminished; just the opposite. Like fans of a winning team or athlete, we slap each other's backs and are inspired, take pride.

On Magic

Do I believe?

Pull a rabbit from a hat? Saw a person in half? Mock birth and death? Fly? Read minds? Pull coins from ears? Turn lead—or straw for that matter—into gold? Appear and disappear at will ("The people here have the strangest way of coming and going!" exclaims Dorothy)?

Magician, Magus, Conjurer, Sorcerer, Wizard, Witch, Elf, Fairy. Shaman. Alchemist. Illusionist. Hypnotist. Artist. Magical realist. Messiah.

Spells and curses!

Merlin. Harry Potter. Gandalf the Gray (or Gay, as Ian McKellen has quipped). Glendower ("I can call spirits from the vasty deep," to which Hotspur replies, "Well so can I, or any man, but will they come when you do call?"). Dr. Marvel. Herr Vogler. Prospero. Houdini, the escape artist. David Copperfield, TV trickster. Magic Johnson (defier of athletic expectations). Wish giver. Witch doctor. Miracle worker. Fairy godmother. Jolly old elf. Deus ex machina. Bipiddy, bopiddy, boo: from scullery maid to princess. Ugly duckling to swan.

And then we have the wannabe Magicians, the Mad Scientists. Dr. Frankenstein with his pregnancy envy. Hawthorne's Alymer, the cosmetician, seeking to perfect his wife. And now cosmetic surgery, facelifts and nosejobs, for manmade, homogenized and youthful looks. Improving on nature! Man trapped in woman's body, or vice versa? No worry, surgery can fix. Cloning. Genetic engineering. Cryogenics (faith in future science). Miracle drugs. Scientific "miracles." Scientia sans sapientia.

Or money as magic. The mystique of riches. Daddy Warbucks. Robber barons and lottery winners. The rich are not like you and me (Fitzgerald); nope, they have more money (Hemingway).

Some magic is illusory and we enjoy its tricks. Some is natural and so-far puzzling, but we're sure can be explained (the paranormal); some, defying natural laws, passes understanding (the supernatural).

Cause for wonder, we say, or for superstition, or religion. The occult. The mystical. Mumbo jumbo. Mojo. Mind reading. Thought control. Tarot cards. Crystal balls. Palm reading. Charms and prayers. Rabbit feet. St. Christophers. Santeria.

Spell-binding beauty.

Love potion #9. Love-in-idleness (aka *Viola tricolor*).

Is the moon a goddess or a lifeless rock that astronauts visit, leaving footprints? In Mark Twain's *A Connecticut Yankee in King Arthur's Court,* the time traveler knows from history that there has been a total eclipse and precisely when and for how long. He dupes his medieval captors by proclaiming he will put out the sun if they don't free him. As the natural phenomenon occurs (and as it passes, once they release him), they revere him as a sorcerer.

The gods must be crazy. A Coke bottle, thrown from an airplane, falls from the Bushman's sky.

Shakespeare's Prospero suggests that magical powers can be acquired from books. He rules his island like Providence, out-witching the evil powers of Sycorax and enslaving her unregenerate son, Caliban, as well as the fairy spirit, Ariel. He commands illusions, storms, sea wrecks, feasts, etc. and puts his past enemies—those who usurped his civil powers—through a kind of reformative therapy; then abjures his magic, breaks his staff and drowns his book.

Faith, despair, love, and rationalism are the themes of Ingmar Bergman's *The Magician* (1958). Albert Vogler once had "healing powers," but now resorts to crude tricks as he tours the nineteenth-century provinces with "Vogler's Magnetic Health Theater." He and his troupe are detained in Stockholm and brought to a Consul's house, where they are challenged by the Minister of Health (Dr. Vergerus) and the Chief of Police to prove they aren't dangerous charlatans and cheats. Supposedly mute, a despairing Vogler privately confides to his transvestite wife: "I hate them, their faces, bodies." During a command performance Vogler is then murdered, seemingly, by a humiliated subject—the Consul's stableman—and skeptical Dr. Vergerus performs the autopsy. In one of the classic scenes in film (https://www.criterion.com/current/posts/2576-repertory-pick-magic-max), both Vergerus and the viewer are terrified by Vogler's seeming ghost. Vogler is alive, of course, an artist begging for money: "I did everything in my power to make you feel something." Is it magic or deceit that defies death?

Gabriel Marquez has less-tormented fun in conflating religion and art in his story, "A Very Old Man with Enormous Wings" (https://www.ndsu.edu/pubweb/~cinichol/CreativeWriting/323/MarquezManwithWings.htm). A decrepit, aged angel is grounded in a peasant family's backyard, and treated first as a carnival attraction by neighbors, investigated by a priest and rejected by the Church for not conforming to its idea of angels, and regarded as an annoyance by the family's wife, even as they prosper from spectator fees. Miracles exist but are treated as mere curiosities, especially if they fail to feed expectations for melodrama and morality.

Both Bergman and Marquez seem nostalgic about earlier ages of faith. I'm unsure about Dostoyevski, as he has the atheist Ivan Karamazov propose a "fantasy," where the Grand Inquisitor threatens to burn the returning Jesus as a heretic (http://www2.hawaii.edu/~freeman/courses/phil100/11.%20Dostoevsky.pdf). "You hoped that, in following you, man too would make do with God, not requiring a miracle. And since man is not strong enough to get by without the miracle, he creates new miracles for himself, his own now, and bows down before the miracle of the quack and the witchcraft of the peasant woman, even though he is a mutineer, heretic, and atheist a hundred times over." Scorning the Church's materialism, Ivan portrays orthodoxy as a deception, meant to elevate the clergy to godhood, while using "miracle, mystery, authority" to relieve mankind of "freedom." As earthly masters, the clergy keeps the inferior masses fed and happy. Only the clergy is strong enough to live knowing there is no heavenly reward, and that "Beyond the tomb, [people] will find only death." Alyosha, an apprentice monk and Ivan's brother, rejects this cynical view and contrasts skepticism throughout the novel with instances of the sacred that do not contradict natural laws but do have transforming power. He counters nihilism with agape love (see Hubert Dreyfus at https://www.youtube.com/watch?v=4YcbhLgftJA).

Apparently Einstein's theory of relativity, a mathematical description that relates spirit and matter, agrees with Judaism's doctrine of Zimzum (https://arxiv.org/ftp/arxiv/papers/0706/0706.4400.pdf).

Magical thinking is "believing in things more strongly than either evidence or experience justifies" (https://www.psychologytoday.com/blog/happiness-in-world/200911/magical-thinking); "it's the feeling that you can control events by wishful thinking: 'The volcano will not erupt if we sacrifice such-and-such.' 'John will come back if I don't give away his shoes'" (Joan Didion).

The saw never touches the woman in the box; her "separated lower half" was a dummy's from the start, while her real legs fit into a hidden compartment. The blood isn't real. Yet seeing is believing. We delight in the performer's suggestion combined with our own cognitive and perceptual flaws. We have "inattention blindness" and "fail to see something [we're] looking at directly if [we're] attending to something else"; we have "unsighted vision" as our "visual system convinces [us] that something is there, when in fact there is just a gap or a missing piece"; and "failure of imagination" as we accept that "there is [nothing] hidden behind the object in the foreground" (https://aeon.co/essays/how-real-magic-happens-when-the-brain-sees-hidden-things).

James Alan McPherson describes magic as freedom from easy classification, color, class and caste. His Virginia Valentine in the 1960s is an avatar of omni-American democracy: "a country raconteur with a stock of stories flavored by international experience ... She was unique. She was a classic kind of narrator ... a magic woman" ("Elbow Room"). As a narrator himself, he casts his spell of humor, learning, pain, tricks and optimism with his stories. Later he writes about his efforts to instill magic in his daughter's life after his divorce. He encourages her imagination in emails and visits. He establishes a ritual of taking her to Disneyland, the Magic Kingdom, and of flying to visit diverse friends. "A belief in the possibility of magic, or of acts of kindly invention, has been one of the sources of our bond during all these years." Together, they imagine a realm that "ministers ... to what is best in people," and "the places at which the rational world, with all its assaults, and the irrational world, with all its potency, meet and dance in some kind of benign compromise about the hidden gods of life and their intentions."

Tim O'Brien's story "Ghost Soldiers" (1990), offers magic as malpractice, which rebounds on the inventor. His fictional soldier in Vietnam, "Tim O'Brien," has been wounded and now seeks revenge on the inexperienced medic who failed to treat his wound properly. As the medic goes on watch one night, O'Brien (now mostly healed and free of combat duty) has rigged an array of special effects—ropes, noisemakers, flares, and tear-gas grenades—outside the medic's bunker and enlisted a sadistic combat buddy, Azar, as his assistant. He wants the medic to feel what he had felt. Their simulated VC attack at first causes the medic to panic. "Now you know," O'Brien thinks. "Together we understood what terror was: you're not human anymore." But the illusion of combat reawakens O'Brien's own panic, his fears of death, conscience, and the boogeyman forces of the VC. It has been blasphemy to invoke it at all. He cringes and begs Azar to stop, but Azar spurns him and redoubles the attack until the medic figures it out and calls O'Brien's name. At that, Azar declares "show's over," labels Tim the "sorriest fuckin case I ever seen," kicks him in the head, and leaves. O'Brien and the medic are left even, "almost war buddies." The medic treats O'Brien's head, congratulates him on his talents and wryly they vow to repay Azar, or kill him. Art runs this risk, the author implies, as does war: beware the knowns and unknowns that you court.

*

Today's wonders, tomorrow's givens. Machines beam back closeup pictures of distant planets as well as our bodies' inscapes. My GPS keeps me found no matter the terrain or destination. MRI-guided radioactive seeds "smart-bomb" cancer cells in my prostate. My sister-in-law undergoes a stem-cell transfusion.

*

How many addictions come from a longing for magic? Booze, gambling, sex, shopping, drugs?

*

Sometimes someone (child, mother, wife, reader) will see me as magical, when I'm not. And once I disappoint, I protest: "What do you want from me? Magic?"

*

We put faith in expertise: the pilot flies the plane, the surgeon operates, the philosopher broods, our grandchildren blindly master iPhones. Historical game changers have been gunpowder, the printing press, the railroad, electricity, aspirin, the car and airplane, the telephone, film, radio and TV, the Bomb, the computer and internet. Some thinkers worry that as artificial intelligence develops, our machines will become smarter than users, smarter even than their inventors. "So how do we respond to all this technological impenetrability?" asks Samuel Arbesman. "One response is to simply give up…[and declare], that everything from light bulbs to vacuum cleaners works via 'magic'.… This intellectual surrender in the face of increasing complexity seems too extreme and even a bit cowardly, but what should we replace it with if we can't understand our creations anymore?"(https://aeon.co/essays/is-technology-making-the-world-indecipherable?).

In Kubrick's Nietzschean film *2001,* the most-advanced HAL (our creation) yields to the Tablet and Star-child.

*

The purest, most astonishing magic that I've ever witnessed—no sleight of hand involved, no illusions—was my wife's delivery of my daughter. The doctor's scalpel, slicing her perineum and blood welling, and then his gloved hands slipping around the crowning baby's, wet, dark-haired skull, and with an expert tug as Connie gave a final push (in meaningful agony), like that, the baby out, umbilical cut, and held by feet, gasping. And Connie's ecstatic gasp, "Oh, look at her!" Nature, yes; and more than nature, also; the rabbit from the hat.

Acknowledgments

The following essays appeared in slightly different forms in *Brevity* ("On Conscience"), *The Massachusetts Review* ("On Weather," "On Cursing"), *Constellations* ("On Falling"), *Plume* ("On Handshakes," "On Silence," "On Empathy"), *Juked* ("On Time," "On Meat"), *Solstice* ("On Privilege"), *LitMag* ("On Bonds"), *The Woven Tale Press* ("On Voice," "On Color"). My thanks to these publications and their editors.

About the Author

DeWitt Henry was the founding editor of *Ploughshares*. He has published a novel, two memoirs, a story collection, and several anthologies. He is a Professor Emeritus at Emerson College and serves as a contributing editor to both *Woven Tale Press* and *Solstice* magazines. For details see dewitthenry.com.